Entrance to the Auschwitz
concentration camp. AKG PHOTO (1986)

Joel Marcus

Jesus and the Holocaust

Reflections
on Suffering
and Hope

DOUBLEDAY

New York   London   Toronto   Sydney   Auckland

PUBLISHED BY DOUBLEDAY
a division of Bantam Doubleday Dell Publishing Group, Inc.
1540 Broadway, New York, New York 10036

DOUBLEDAY and the portrayal of an anchor with a dolphin
are trademarks of Doubleday, a division
of Bantam Doubleday Dell Publishing Group, Inc.

The "July 15, 1944 entry from *The Diary of Anne Frank: The Critical
Edition* by Anne Frank. Copyright © 1986 by Anne Frank-Fonds,
Basel/Switzerland, for all texts of Anne Frank. Used by permission
of Doubleday, a division of Bantam Doubleday Dell
Publishing Group, Inc.

Book Design by Paul Randall Mize

Library of Congress Cataloging-in-Publication Data

Marcus, Joel, 1951–
Jesus and the Holocaust : reflections on suffering and hope
Joel Marcus. — 1st ed.
p. cm.
Includes bibliographical references (p. 137).
1. Good Friday sermons.   2. Jesus Christ—Crucifixion—Sermons.
3. Holocaust (Christian theology).   4. Sermons, American.   I. Title.
BV4276.M37   1997
231.7'6—dc21   96-48352
CIP

To Peter and Denise Francis

Acknowledgments

I AM GRATEFUL to my friend Peter Francis, the provost of St. Mary's Cathedral in Glasgow, for inviting me to arrange the service and encouraging me to publish the homilies. Thanks for encouragement and advice also go to my Glasgow colleagues John Riches and John Barclay, and to Denise Francis, Cleo Kearns, Lou Martyn, Bruce Ward, and my mother, Frances Marcus. I am also grateful to Mark Fretz, my editor at Doubleday, for his enthusiasm about the project and for his help in shaping up the manuscript for publication.

Most biblical citations are from the New Revised Standard Version, with only minor alterations here and there; in one or two cases I have preferred the more literal rendering of the RSV or my own translation from the original Hebrew or Greek text.

Contents

Illustrations

Preface

WHEN I LIVED in New York City in the 1970s, one of the elevator men in my apartment building was a Holocaust survivor from Hungary. He was a man of great physical strength, with thick, muscular forearms, on one of which was tattooed his registration number from the concentration camp. He also had a quality of Old World courtliness that set him apart, not only from the other elevator men but also from most other people I knew. I remember thinking that one would have needed strength to survive the camps; his bodily vitality, therefore, did not surprise me. But his courtesy did.

I can recall only one occasion upon which that courtesy failed. The television mini-series "Holocaust" was being aired for the first time, and one night I asked Walter whether or not he was watching it. A shadow seemed to pass over his face, and he shook his head, not making eye contact. "No one who hasn't been through it can know what it was like," he said, and then fell silent. I couldn't think of anything to say either, so we rode up to my floor wordlessly and awkwardly. He opened the door, and I got out; without saying his usual "good night," he shut the door again, and the elevator moved off.

In spite of such an unforgettable warning, and the depth of feeling it conveyed, I have nevertheless tried to say something meaningful about the Holocaust in the pages that follow. I have not done so because I think I possess the ultimate "answer" to it. These pages, rather, bear witness to a very particular occasion. Two years ago I was asked to preach at the Good Friday service at the Episcopal cathedral in Glasgow. This service lasts from noon to 3 P.M., the traditional hour of Jesus' death (Mark 15:34), and it recalls and invites the congregation to reflect upon the meaning of that death through readings from the Bible and other literature, through music, through prayer, and through preaching.

Under any circumstances, the planning of such a service is a major undertaking. For me in April 1995, however, the job was doubly challenging because of the coming together of world history with my own past. The historical factor is that the spring of 1995 was a time for commemorating the fiftieth anniversary of the end of the Holocaust. The personal factor is that I myself am of Jewish parentage, brought up in a secular Jewish home in a Chicago suburb. In my early twenties I became a Christian, and later a New Testament scholar; but I continue to view myself as a Jew. (This opinion, incidentally, is shared by Jewish law.)

Since my area of scholarly expertise is the New Testament Gospels, I decided to preach on the portrait of Jesus' suffering and death in each of them. But in view of the historical moment in which the service was taking place, I also decided to try to explore the links between that one Jewish death and the six million Jewish deaths that occurred more than nineteen hundred years later. I wanted to see if the hope that Christians have always found hidden in the darkest hour of their liturgical year might shed any light on the most tragic moment of our recent history—and vice versa.

No, I do not really know what the Holocaust was like. I don't know what it's like to see my child, or my parent, or my friend swept off to death or murdered before my eyes (God grant that I may never know). But neither do I know exactly how a crucifixion feels. Yet on Good Friday one says something about crucifixion. And in the fiftieth year after the end of the Holocaust, one says something about the Holocaust. And when those two things come together, one tries, however inadequately, to say something about their mysterious relation to each other.

I

The Suffering Servant

Marc Chagall, *The Crucified,* 1944. LAUROS-GIRAUDON

The Secret Mission

[IN THE LITHUANIAN SHTETL or town of Eisysky, the Jewish population of four thousand was liquidated on September 25, 1941.] In groups of 250, first the men and then the women, the people were taken to the old Jewish cemetery in front of the open ditches. They were ordered to undress and stand at the edge of the open graves. They were shot in the back of the head by Lithuanian guards with the encouragement and help of the local people. The chief executioner was the Lithuanian Ostrovakas. Dressed in a uniform, a white apron, and gloves, he personally supervised the killing. He reserved for himself the privilege of shooting the town's notables . . . and he practiced sharpshooting at the children, aiming as they were thrown into the graves.

Among the Jews that September 25, 1941, in the old Jewish cemetery of Eisysky was one of the shtetl's melamdim [teachers], Reb Michalowsky, and his youngest son, Zvi, age sixteen. Father and son were holding hands as they stood naked at the edge of the open pit, trying to comfort each other during their

last moments. Young Zvi was counting the bullets
and the intervals between one volley of fire and the
next. As Ostrovakas and his people were aiming their
guns, Zvi fell into the grave a split second before the
volley of fire hit him.

He felt the bodies piling up on top of him and
covering him. He felt the streams of blood around him
and the trembling pile of dying bodies moving beneath him.

It became cold and dark. The shooting died down
above him. Zvi made his way from under the bodies,
out of the mass grave into the cold, dead night. In the
distance, Zvi could hear Ostrovakas and his people
singing and drinking, celebrating their great accomplishment. After 800 years, on September 26, 1941,
Eisysky was *Judenfrei* [cleansed of Jews].

At the far end of the cemetery, in the direction of
the huge church, were a few Christian homes. Zvi
knew them all. Naked, covered with blood, he
knocked on the first door. The door opened. A peasant
was holding a lamp which he had looted earlier in the
day from a Jewish home. "Please let me in," Zvi
pleaded. The peasant lifted the lamp and examined
the boy closely. "Jew, go back to the grave where you
belong!" he shouted at Zvi and slammed the door in
his face. Zvi knocked on other doors, but the response
was the same.

Near the forest lived a widow whom Zvi knew too.
He decided to knock on her door. The old widow

opened the door. She was holding in her hand a small, burning piece of wood. "Let me in!" begged Zvi. "Jew, go back to the grave at the old cemetery!" She chased Zvi away with the burning piece of wood as if exorcising an evil spirit, a dybbuk.

"I am your Lord, Jesus Christ. I came down from the cross. Look at me—the blood, the pain, the suffering of the innocent. Let me in," said Zvi Michalowsky. The widow crossed herself and fell at his blood-stained feet. *"Boże moj, Boże moj* (my God, my God)," she kept crossing herself and praying. The door was opened.

Zvi walked in. He promised her that he would bless her children, her farm, and her, but only if she would keep his visit a secret for three days and three nights and not reveal it to a living soul, not even the priest. She gave Zvi food and clothing and warm water to wash himself. Before leaving the house, he once more reminded her that the Lord's visit must remain a secret, because of His special mission on earth.

Dressed in a farmer's clothing, with a supply of food for a few days, Zvi made his way to the nearby forest. Thus, the Jewish partisan movement was born in the vicinity of Eisysky.

—From Yaffa Eliach, *Hasidic Tales of the Holocaust,* pp. 53–55

A Reading from the Book of the Prophet Isaiah

Who has believed what we have heard?
  And to whom has the arm of the LORD been
    revealed?
For he grew up before him like a young plant,
  and like a root out of dry ground;
he had no form or majesty that we should look at
    him,
  nothing in his appearance that we should desire
    him.
He was despised and rejected by people,
  a man of sorrows and acquainted with infirmity;
and as one from whom folk hide their faces
  he was despised, and we held him of no account.

Surely he has borne our infirmities
  and carried our diseases;
yet we accounted him stricken,
  struck down by God, and afflicted.
But he was wounded for our transgressions,
  crushed for our iniquities;

upon him was the punishment that made us whole,
  and by his bruises we are healed.
All we like sheep have gone astray;
  we have all turned to our own way;
and the Lord has laid on him
  the iniquity of us all.

He was oppressed, and he was afflicted,
  yet he did not open his mouth
  like a lamb that is led to the slaughter,
and like a sheep that before its shearers is silent,
  so he did not open his mouth.
By a perversion of justice he was taken away;
  Who could have imagined his future?
For he was cut off from the land of the living,
  stricken for the transgression of my people.
They made his grave with the wicked
  and his tomb with the rich,
although he had done no violence,
  and there was no deceit in his mouth.

Yet it was the will of the LORD to crush him with
      pain.
When you make his life an offering for sin,
  he shall see his offspring, and shall prolong his
      days;
through him the will of the LORD shall prosper.
Out of his anguish he shall see the light;
  he shall find satisfaction through his knowledge.

The righteous one, my servant, shall make many
    righteous,
    and he shall bear their iniquities.
Therefore I will allot him a portion with the great,
    and he shall divide the spoil with the strong;
because he poured out himself to death,
    and was numbered with the transgressors;
yet he bore the sin of many,
    and made intercession for the transgressors.
    (Isaiah 53:1–12)

THIS TEXT, the fifty-third chapter of Isaiah, has from the beginnings of the Church been considered to be one of the most important prophecies of the suffering and atoning death of Christ. I can still remember my own shock the first time I read it, during the years when I was beginning to become interested in Christianity after an upbringing in a secularized Jewish home. Prior to this, I had encountered the idea of Jesus' atoning death only on church signboards and roadside signs: "Christ died for your sins." I had always wondered about this strange sentence. Wasn't sin a rather antiquated, nineteenth-century concept? And even if one accepted the notion that there was such a thing, how could one person die for *another's* sins? But here was this same puzzling concept, not in the New Testament, but in the Old.

The passage seemed transparently to speak of the suffering and death of an innocent man, God's righteous servant, as an atonement for the sins of his people. This man was despised and rejected by other people, and a man of sorrows; he suffered, and his sufferings were considered by others to be proof that he had been smitten by God. But in reality, Isaiah tells us, his suffering and death were for the benefit of his people: "He was wounded for our transgressions, crushed for our iniquities; upon him was the punishment that made us whole, and by his bruises we are healed." Even from what little I knew of Christian theology, this sounded frighteningly close to the way in which Christians spoke about Jesus' death. What, I wondered, was this Christian text doing in the Jewish part of the Bible?

I did not immediately go out and ask for a second opinion from a rabbi, but if I had done so I probably would have gotten a very different view of Isaiah 53. For the standard Jewish position on this passage has been to deny that it speaks of the suffering of an individual, still less of the suffering of the Messiah. Rather, in the usual Jewish view, the Lord's suffering servant is a collective figure. Specifically, he is the nation of Israel, the physical descendants of Abraham—the Jews, who are persecuted, harassed, and killed by the surrounding nations, yet who mysteriously become the instrument for their redemption.

Needless to say, Christians down through the centuries have not been happy with this interpretation. For two thousand years, therefore, Christians and Jews have been arguing about Isaiah's words, and some of the arguments have not been pretty. They were especially ugly during the Middle Ages, when Christians had the upper hand politically, and often forced Jews to engage in public disputations about Isaiah 53 and other Old Testament texts. The Jews were caught in a very uncomfortable position: if they lost the argument, they could be forced to convert to Christianity, but if they held their ground and refused to accept the Christian interpretation, they could be banished or subjected to other forms of persecution.

So who is right, the Jews or the Christians? Does Isaiah 53 refer to the atoning death of a suffering individual, or does it refer to the atoning death of a suffering group? Most modern scholars would admit that there is evidence to support both interpretations. On the one hand, the Servant seems in our passage to have a mission to Israel, and that suggests that he is an individual separate from Israel. On the other hand, elsewhere in this section of Isaiah the Lord's Servant *is* explicitly identified as Israel. A few chapters before ours, for example, the author addresses Israel in these terms: "But now hear, O Jacob, my servant, and Israel, whom I have chosen" (Isaiah 44:1).

So who is right? The wisest theological course may be to affirm that the Lord's Servant is *both* Israel and her suffering Messiah. In saying this, I am keenly aware of how important texts like Isaiah 53, which speak of innocent suffering, continue to be for Jews, especially since the Holocaust. Jewish exegetes and theologians say, "When Isaiah speaks of the Lord's Servant being despised and rejected by people, he is speaking of us, who were branded as subhuman, not only by common opinion, but by law. When we hear him describe the way in which folk hid their faces from the Servant, we recall how we were turned away by our neighbors when we knocked at their doors and pleaded with them to hide us from the Gestapo, and how afterward they claimed that they didn't know what had happened to us. When he describes the Servant being led like a lamb to the slaughter, we recall our parents, our spouses, and our children, who filed so silently to the gas chambers, not daring to open their mouths." In 1995, this year of commemorations, a half-century from the end of World War II and the final extinguishing of the crematoria, we dare not disregard these voices.

But neither, I think, should Christians give up their insistence that Jesus' redemptive suffering on the cross is being spoken of in Isaiah 53. Might there not be a way to combine these two interpretations? Might one not suggest that there is an analogy, a likeness, a mysterious identification between the redemptive sufferings of Jesus and the sufferings of other innocent victims, including Holocaust victims? After all, Paul himself says in Colossians (1:24) that he makes up what is lacking in Christ's sufferings. And even some Jewish writers and artists have expressed a similar sort of intuition of an identification between Christ's sufferings and that of the martyrs of the Holocaust. One thinks, for example, of the crucifixion scenes painted by Marc Chagall in the late thirties and early forties— scenes in which the crucified one is always an identifiably Jewish figure, and the background is usually a burning Jewish settlement or shtetl of Eastern Europe.

Of this series of crucifixion paintings, the most affecting is the last, called simply *The Crucified* (see page 18). It is described by David Roskies in these terms:

> Fully clothed Russian Jews hang on a series of crosses. The town is blanketed by snow. A corpse lies on the doorstep on the right, a slaughtered hen lies in the center, and a dead mother with an infant at her breast (a familiar motif) lies on the left. Chagall achieves a greater sense of desecration here, because both sky and earth are barren; there is a multiplicity of crosses, and the crucified Jews at every other doorstep suggest a symbolic inversion of the Passover: no Angel of Death passes over the Israelite houses marked with blood—instead, the hands of an enemy have nailed the Jews to individual crosses in front of their houses. It is therefore a landscape abandoned by God—but not entirely by man. A benign human presence still remains in the *Judenrein* [Jew-free] shtetl, none other than King David playing his harp, who is a symbol of the artist himself. This refusal on Chagall's part to abandon his town, his past, and his people to the

forces of destruction is the sign of his faith in the redemptive powers of art.

Roskies's interpretation is insightful in many ways, but can the landscape really be said to be "abandoned by God"? The softly shimmering figure of the harpist sitting on the rooftop, which does not draw the observer's eye away from the crucified figures and yet looms benignly over them is, as he acknowledges, a symbol of a redemptive power. And I doubt that, for Chagall, that redemptive power is only the power of art. Indeed, if the figure really *is* meant to be King David, who lived and died so many hundreds of years ago, then his presence speaks in some way of life beyond the grave.

Certainly Roskies is right that, for Chagall in this painting, there is no God "out there," away in the sky, but that does not mean that God has disappeared altogether. He is not off somewhere in the sky because he has come down and become, so to speak, incarnate in the figure of the harpist, who balances miraculously on the chimney of the snowy shtetl house. And if the crucifixion of Jesus is mirrored in the crucifixions of the Russian Jews on their crosses, then Jesus' resurrection is also perhaps echoed in the portrayal of the similarly clad Russian Jewish David playing his harp and thus somehow bestowing a blessing upon the sad scene.

There is, of course, a terrible irony in such a suggestion, since Jews have been persecuted down through the ages as the supposed killers of Christ. Indeed, Holy Week has always been a particularly dangerous time for Jews for this very reason, for it is then especially that Christian mobs have gone on the rampage against their Jewish neighbors out of revenge for their alleged crime of murdering God. In this light we can understand why, for many Jews, the cross stands not so much for the death of Jesus nearly two thousand years ago as for the deaths, down through the ages, of the Jewish men, women, and children who have been murdered in Jesus' name. *That* is why songs like "Onward Christian Soldiers," or even the sight of a cross, can turn Jewish stomachs. Not because Jews intrinsically hate Jesus, but because of the things that have been done in his name.

If, in spite of all this sordid history, Chagall can still depict Jewish crucifixions and Chaim Potok can write a novel about a Hasidic artist who paints similar scenes and Martin Buber can embrace Jesus as an elder brother and Geza Vermes can write books about the religion of Jesus the Jew—well then, that is testimony to the amazing power of Jesus to break through human misunderstanding and to present himself anew, unshackled from human preconceptions, to each generation.

And such breakthroughs happen not only in art and scholarship, but also in areas more directly involved in life. Consider, for example, Yaffa Eliach's true story of

Zvi, the Jewish boy who claimed to be Jesus come down from the cross. On one level, of course, this story describes the trick that enabled a quick-witted youth to escape from certain death by exploiting the gullibility of a superstitious old woman. But this tale, like other stories in Eliach's remarkable book, may also become a parable of something more—of a likeness which can, depending on the circumstances, be exploited to save a life, dimly intuited through a veil of superstition, or humbly acknowledged with genuine faith.

This, then, is the theme that we will explore together: the likeness between the suffering and death of Jesus on the cross and the suffering and death of his relatives according to the flesh during the Nazi era. It goes without saying that others besides Jews suffered under Hitler's oppression, and that millions of other innocent people have had their lives snuffed out by human cruelty since World War II. But this is a special time of commemoration for the Holocaust, and it is fitting that we should link it with the death of Jesus, which we commemorate on Good Friday. Because despite all the misunderstanding and hatred that has characterized relations between Christians and Jews for nearly two thousand years, stories such as that of Zvi Michalowsky may point toward other chapters yet to be written in the long and tortured history of the Jewish people's relationship to Jesus of Nazareth.

And perhaps some of these chapters will involve further extraordinary unfoldings of the meaning of Isaiah 53: when God makes the Servant's life an offering for sin, "he shall see his offspring, and shall prolong his days; through him the will of the Lord shall prosper."

II

*"You Are Being
Dehumanized"*

Shoes confiscated from Holocaust victims,
Majdanek death camp. ARNOLD CRAMER

Isaac

At dawn, the sun strolled in the forest
Together with me and father,
And my right hand was in his left.

Like lightning a knife flashed among the trees.
And I am so afraid of my eyes' terror, faced by
    blood on the leaves.

Father, father, quickly save Isaac
So that no one will be missing at the midday meal.

It is I who am being slaughtered, my son,
And already my blood is on the leaves.
And father's voice was smothered
And his face was pale.

And I wanted to scream, writhing not to believe,
And tearing open my eyes.
And I woke up.

And my right hand was drained of blood.

—Amir Gilboa, in *The Penguin Book of Hebrew
Verse,* p. 56

A Reading from the Gospel According to Mark

Then they brought Jesus to the place called Golgotha (which means the place of a skull). And they offered him wine mixed with myrrh; but he did not take it. And they crucified him, and divided his clothes among them, casting lots to decide who should take what. It was nine o'clock in the morning, and they crucified him. The inscription of the charge against him read, "The King of the Jews." And with him they crucified two bandits, one on his right and one on his left. (Mark 15:22–27)

IN A FAMOUS ESSAY, Erich Auerbach contrasts the biblical mode of storytelling with that found in classical Greek literature such as Homer's *Odyssey*. The *Odyssey* delights in detail, in descriptions of physical appearance, including descriptions of the gods, in explicit accounts of physical settings and of actions that reveal character in an unambiguous way. Biblical narrative, on the other hand, is spare and lacking in detail. What is most important is often left unexpressed, for the reader to puzzle out.

In the account of Abraham's near-sacrifice of his son Isaac, for example, no description is initially given of why God decided to command the sacrifice, nor of where Abraham was when he received the terrible order. Nor are we told how Abraham knows that the voice that speaks to him is that of God rather than that of a deceitful demon. The voice of God comes to him from some invisible, unimaginable depth, and he obeys it. We do not hear about Abraham's emotions— neither what he feels during his three-day journey with Isaac to the place where he is to sacrifice him; nor what passes through his mind when Isaac asks him why they have no lamb for the burnt offering; nor what he or Isaac is thinking during the moments when he builds an altar, binds Isaac to it, and lifts the knife to kill him. We are not even told what they go through when, at the last moment, a voice from heaven prevents the slaughter of Isaac. Did the experience leave a permanent scar, whether physical or emotional, on either of them? Did Isaac subsequently hesitate if Abraham asked him to go on a trip with him again? All this is left in darkness, yet some understanding of it is critical to our perception of the narrative. Readers must fill in these crucial gaps through their own knowledge and conjectures; the biblical narrative is, as Auerbach puts it, "fraught with background."

Indeed, this narrative is so fraught that down through the ages interpreters have consciously or unconsciously read their own concerns and experiences into it. In ancient and medieval times, Jewish exegetes saw Isaac as a symbol of the Jewish people, called upon to offer themselves up to death for the sake of the God who was supposed to love them and to have chosen them to be his elect nation. In some Jewish versions of the story, Isaac becomes a grown man who willingly sacrifices himself and is then miraculously restored to life, and his death becomes an atoning sacrifice; these versions may provide part of the background to the New Testament idea of Jesus' sacrificial death. In the modern era, Wilfred Owen retold the tale in such a way that Abraham's hand was not stayed, and the poet, a British officer in World War I, linked the murder with the senseless carnage he saw all around him, which soon claimed his own life; despite the angel's warning not to harm the boy, "the old man would not so, but slew his son, / and half the seed of Europe, one by one." The Jewish poet Amir Gilboa gave the story a different twist to reflect his own experience during the Holocaust, in which his father died (see *The Penguin Book of Hebrew Verse*, p. xx); in this version the son pleads not to be slaughtered, and the father, pale-faced, replies that he himself is being killed instead, "and already my blood is on the leaves." The ending of the poem conveys the nightmarish guilt of the survivor: the boy lives, but his subsequent existence is only a half-life, since he has deposited a significant part of himself in the grave with his beloved parent; his right hand, which had been holding his father's hand, is now drained of blood.

Like the Old Testament story of the sacrifice of Isaac, the Gospel narrative of Jesus' crucifixion is also "fraught with background." What was going through Jesus' mind as he was driven to Golgotha? Why did he not carry his own cross? What was he feeling as he reached the place of execution, as he was stripped of his clothes, as he was laid on the cross? Was he conscious throughout the entire procedure, or did he faint? How was he fastened to the cross—by ropes, nails, or a combination of the two? Did his crucifixion cause him piercing, unspeakable agony, or was he so exhausted and numbed by the tortures he had already endured that he scarcely noticed it? The narrative does not tell us.

In their sparseness of detail the biblical accounts contrast with many modern reconstructions of Jesus' crucifixion. When I was a kid, for example, I read Lew Wallace's *Ben-Hur,* which had just been made into a major motion picture. I still remember the profound impact that Wallace's graphic description of the crucifixion made on me. I shuddered, fascinated, as I read over and over the description of the cruel nails going through the tender skin of Jesus' palms. Of this sort of gory detail, however, the Gospels tell us nothing.

But presumably some of the first readers of the various Gospels had themselves witnessed crucifixions, and many had probably heard about them. They could, therefore, fill in some of the details of the picture through their own knowledge. We, however, are not so lucky, or unlucky. Still, we are not totally without resources for filling in the background with which the crucifixion account is fraught. We are aided by the continuing history of humans acting horrifically toward each other. While the details of torture and execution have changed over the years, the principles remain the same.

In the Holocaust, for example, victims were, like Jesus, stripped of their clothes before being executed. This was partly, as in the case of Jesus, for the economic benefit of the executioners. The piles of luggage, garments, shoes, jewelry, and eyeglasses discovered at the killing centers bear silent witness to this plunder. Perhaps most haunting are the heaps of shoes which one can see at the Holocaust Museum in Washington—shoes which, in their worn soles, scuffed leather, and frayed laces, seem to retain a portion of the personality of their vanished owners.

"I Saw a Mountain," a poem by Moses Schulstein, movingly captures the impression created by such a pile of shoes at the death camp of Majdanek in Poland. Remarkably, in spite of everything he has seen, the poet still seems to believe that God exists and is actively involved in the world. The pile of shoes collected at Majdanek, higher than Mount Blanc, is not a gigantic garbage dump demonstrating the callousness of humanity, but a mountain more holy than Sinai. And, in Schulstein's vision, the animated shoes of the murdered Jewish men, women, and children refuse to lie quietly on top of each other, but arrange themselves in rows and march off with "steps that measure out the judgment." This same intuition that, in spite of everything, some divine purpose is operative in this crazy universe, leads Mark to quote an Old Testament scripture in describing the Roman soldiers' expropriation of Jesus' clothes: "They divided his clothes among them, casting lots for them, to decide who should take what" (Mark 15:24; cf. Psalm 22:18). God must still be in control, for even the way in which Jesus was stripped and had his clothes raffled off fulfilled the scriptures.

But there was another dimension of the stripping of Holocaust prisoners besides the appropriation and exploitation of people's most personal possessions. This stripping also involved deliberate humiliation. The Jewish tradition was not as liberated as the Greek tradition about the human body. There were no "adult beaches" in ancient Israel, so far as we know, or if there were, they were frowned upon by the authorities. Nakedness, rather, is usually synonymous with disgrace in the Bible and in Jewish tradition. To strip a Jewish prisoner naked, therefore, was to expose him or her to public shame.

This feature of Judaism, by the way, has been recently brought to the fore by a controversy concerning a display at Yad Vashem, the Holocaust museum in Jerusalem. For twenty-five years the museum has displayed photographs taken by the Nazis—who proudly and meticulously documented every step in the killing process. Some of these pictures show Jewish women who have been stripped naked prior to being gassed. Now some ultra-Orthodox Holocaust survivors are insisting that the photos be removed out of respect for the women pictured, because their nakedness, it is claimed, is a shame and blasphemes their memory. Other survivors insist that the shame belongs to the Nazis, not to their victims, and that the photos should remain as a witness to what their sisters, mothers, and friends endured.

As in the case of Jesus, then, the stripping of the victims before execution was deliberately designed not only to make subsequent disposal of their bodies easier but also to humiliate them and thus to force them to submit more docilely to the machinery of extermination. This process of intentional humiliation, indeed, permeated all aspects of concentration camp life, even for those prisoners who were allowed, temporarily, to live on as slave laborers. One survivor, for example, describes his arrival at Auschwitz as a teenager. He made it through selection—the fearsome process by which the arriving prisoners were sorted into two lines, a long line going to immediate death in the gas chambers, a short one going to slave labor and eventual death through starvation, disease, or execution.

Like the other "lucky ones," this young man immediately had his arm tattooed with a number. As he was given his number, an SS man came up to him. "Do you know what this number's all about?" he asked. "No, sir," the youth replied. "Okay, let me tell you now," the SS man said. "You are being dehumanized."

"You are being dehumanized." Torturers are not usually so candid and explicit, but that is what they are about. Before a person can be killed, he or she must be turned into an object—stripped of humanity and reconstituted in the tormentor's mind as something filthy, fit only to be gotten out of the way, eradicated, liquidated. This metamorphosis is what Nazi propaganda films accomplished so brilliantly when they juxtaposed photographs of stereotypical Jews with shots of swarming rats and insects: they divested the Jews of their human qualities, symbolically transferring them from the sphere of neighborly concern into the bailiwick of the exterminator. Alexander Solzhenitsyn alludes to a similar process of methodical dehumanization when he describes the Soviet prison network in bitterly ironic terms as "our sewage disposal system."

And it is precisely this sort of dehumanization that Jesus experienced on the cross—for our benefit. He was flushed away in the ancient Roman sewage disposal system. And this means that none of our lostness, none of our feeling of worthlessness, none of our sensation of dehumanization is strange to him. Does not the speaker in Psalm 22, the same psalm that describes the raffling of his clothes, and a psalm that the Church has always interpreted as a prophecy of Christ's suffering, say, "I am a worm, not human" (Psalm 22:6)? The bitterness, the lostness, the despair of this statement cannot, must not, be denied to Jesus, or we are deprived of our one true hope when we become as worms in our own eyes.

For we must grasp the radical nature of the incarnation, which is nowhere better expressed than in certain declarations of St. Paul. Christ became a curse for us (Galatians 3:13). God made him, who did not know sin, to become sin, in order that we might become the righteousness of God in him (2 Corinthians 5:21). Note that both of these extraordinary statements seem to describe a Christ who has been stripped of his human identity and reduced to the status of an object, the most detestable kind imaginable. For Paul does not say that Christ became a cursed person, but that he became *a curse;* he does not say that God turned him into a sinful human being, but that he turned him into *sin.* Christ became a *thing* for us—a *bad* thing. When we feel, therefore, that the negative opinion of other people, or their indifference, or our own failings have robbed us of our most precious possession, our image of ourselves as worthwhile human beings, we are not undergoing an experience that is alien to Christ.

And it is precisely in this ability to identify ourselves with Jesus, or rather in his self-identification with our dehumanized state, that our humanity is returned to us. Christ becomes sin, but we become the righteousness *of God in him,* so that our personhood is revived in a double way: through the fullness of God's restorative personality and through the vital, all-inclusive human personhood of Christ.

One might try to avoid the radical force of these terrible and wonderful Pauline statements by claiming that they are only metaphorical. As Emmanuel Levinas points out, however, it is a principle of Jewish exegesis that in many cases "the literal meaning leads further than the metaphor." And so it is here. It would be misguided to try, as some have done, to save Jesus' dignity by claiming that, while he certainly endured physical torture on the cross, he never descended into the pit of self-doubt and hopelessness, of radical lostness before God, that so often characterizes us. For if Jesus was spared such an experience, why, I wonder, did he cry out on the cross, "My God, my God, why have you forsaken me?"

III

An Atheist in Five Minutes

Margit Ullrichová (1931–1944), Theresienstadt,
Child and Autumm Trees. JEWISH MUSEUM, PRAGUE

There's a Certain Slant of Light

There's a certain Slant of light,
Winter Afternoons—
That oppresses, like the Heft
Of Cathedral Tunes—

Heavenly Hurt, it gives us—
We can find no scar,
But internal difference,
Where the Meanings, are—

None may teach it—Any—
'Tis the Seal Despair—
An imperial affliction
Sent us of the Air—

When it comes, the Landscape listens—
Shadows—hold their breath—
When it goes, 'tis like the Distance
On the look of Death—

—From Emily Dickinson, *The Complete Poems of
Emily Dickinson,* #268

Glorified and sanctified be God's great name throughout the world which he has created according to his
will. May he establish his kingdom, hastening his salvation and the coming of his Messiah, in your lifetime
and during your days, and within the life of the entire
house of Israel, speedily and soon; and say, Amen.

  —From the Mourner's Kaddish, *Daily Prayer
  Book: Sephardic,* p. 16

A Reading from the Gospel According to Mark

Those who passed by derided him, shaking their heads and saying, "Aha! You who would destroy the temple and build it in three days, save yourself, and come down from the cross!" In the same way the chief priests, along with the scribes, were also mocking him among themselves and saying, "He saved others; he cannot save himself. Let the Messiah, the King of Israel, come down from the cross now, so that we may see and believe." Those who were crucified with him also taunted him. (Mark 15:29–32)

THERE ARE THOSE for whom the Holocaust signals the death of God. It is no longer possible to believe in a God who allows such atrocities to happen. They might apply to the Holocaust Emily Dickinson's words about the unsurpassability of the revelation of the vacuum at the core of the universe: "None may teach it—Any— /'Tis the Seal Despair." Despair is the seal, the final word, the beginning and end of all wisdom.

Despair oozes from some of the paintings by the children of the Theresienstadt concentration camp, such as the watercolor by Margit Ullrichová reproduced on page 50. Here an indistinct figure, who wears a childish hat and probably represents Margit herself, tries to catch one of the leaves that is being shed by a tree in autumn. It is not really clear whether she will be successful—perhaps she will, perhaps not. But what does it really matter? The leaves are dying, they are falling to the ground one by one. Just as Margit's friends and relatives are doing, just as Margit herself will soon do. The last word, the seal, is despair—"An imperial affliction / Sent us of the Air."

And nothing can induce despair more quickly than a premature, ill-thought-out affirmation of faith. A former inmate of Auschwitz says that he became an atheist in five minutes. He was standing next to another man, and they were both gazing at the smoke billowing out of the crematoria chimneys. Finally the other man spoke up: "Well, I suppose all this must have been God's will." And the first man was instantly transformed into an atheist.

Everything depends on how one's faith is expressed. To say in a nonchalant way, "It must have been God's will" when confronted by the enormity of such horrors can kill another person's faith, or even, eventually, one's own. On the other hand, to persevere in faith even when one is in an agony of doubt, to express one's faith implicitly, even without saying anything, may be to maintain it and perhaps to win others to it.

Perhaps this is why Mark does not come right out and *say* explicitly, in his crucifixion and death scenes, that what was happening to Jesus was a fulfillment of scripture. This point has certainly been made earlier in the Gospel, above all by Jesus' prophecies of his suffering and death, in which he has said repeatedly that these torments are "necessary" (Mark 8:31; 9:31; 10:33–34). Why are they necessary? Because God has planned them, and they have been prophesied in the scriptures. Even when Jesus is arrested, he says, "Let the scriptures be fulfilled." But now, in the crucifixion and death scenes themselves, there is no such explicit notice that scripture is being fulfilled. This is unlike the situation in the Gospel of John, where the evangelist three times steps out of his role as reporter of the crucifixion events to tell the reader explicitly, "This happened so that the scripture might be fulfilled" (19:24, 28, 36–37).

In Mark and the other Synoptic Gospels, by contrast, the point is made indirectly, without blaring trumpets calling attention to it. Yet for those with a knowledge of the Old Testament, it would be plain that what was happening to Jesus was, mysteriously, a recapitulation of the experiences of the innocent sufferer who speaks in some of the psalms. If the passion narrative is "fraught with background," then a large part of that background is provided by the Old Testament—which, of course, was the only "scripture" that the early Christians possessed.

Especially important for the scene of Jesus' crucifixion and death is Psalm 22, which begins with the words, "My God, my God, why have you forsaken me?" These words, of course, are repeated by Jesus on the cross. The psalmist goes on to describe the way in which he is mocked by those around him, who wag their heads at him and say, "Let God deliver him, for he trusted in him!" Jesus is mocked in almost identical terms in our passage. And later on in the psalm, we read, "They divided my garments among them, and for my raiment they cast lots"—just as Jesus' garments are divided and raffled off.

Yet Mark and Matthew and Luke do not explicitly make these points. They presume that their hearers know the Old Testament and will recognize from their narrative that scripture is being fulfilled; readers themselves must make the connection rather than having it imposed upon them. Leaving it to the hearers to fill in the gaps in this way can make the point all the more powerfully. The author does not beat readers over the head with his idea: "Things happened in this way because it was God's will, as laid out in the scriptures—and you'd better believe it!" Rather, they independently discover the idea, and it therefore becomes their own; a powerful collusion is thereby created between author and insightful readers.

So, are the suffering, humiliation, and despair that

Jesus experiences on the cross the will of God? Was the Holocaust the will of God? To deny that these terrible events are God's will is to leave the door open to an even more terrifying possibility—that the world has slipped off the rails and is no longer in God's control. But to say in an assertive, arrogant, un-nuanced way that they *are* God's will is to run the risk of turning all of us instantly into atheists. Perhaps, when faced with such a question, we can do only what Matthew, Mark, and Luke do: allude, hint, suggest, leaving open the possibility that these terrible events somehow reflect the will of a gracious God.

But if God's will is being fulfilled through Jesus' death, it is being fulfilled in a terribly ironic way. Irony, indeed, is a feature that runs all through the passion narrative, especially in Mark. People say and do things that hint at truths far deeper than they themselves realize. The Roman soldiers, for example, put royal apparel on Jesus and kneel before him say-ing, "Hail, King of the Jews!" (Mark 15:17–18); the chief priests, similarly, proclaim, "Let the Christ, the king of Israel, come down from the cross now, so that we may see and believe" (Mark 15:31–32). Neither group, of course, really believes that Jesus is the king of Israel; their acknowledgment of his kingship is a mocking one. Yet for the readers, who *do* believe in Jesus' messiahship, his enemies' calling him "king of Israel" is unwitting testimony to his status.

Indeed, in a very subtle way, Mark has been laying

the groundwork for this mockery of Jesus' kingship throughout this entire chapter of the Gospel. In Mark the term "king" is never applied to Jesus until the beginning of Chapter 15, when he stands before Pontius Pilate; then, in the trial before Pilate, the subsequent mockery, and the crucifixion scene, it is applied to him six times within the space of thirty verses. Although all of these usages of "king" are either skeptical, as when Pilate asks Jesus if he is the king of the Jews, or sarcastic, as when the religious leaders mock the crucified Jesus as "the king of Israel," Mark's readers are expected to see the ironic truth behind them. There are even subtler hints for discerning readers; the narrative, for example, portrays Jesus "enthroned" between two bandits, as kings were often portrayed enthroned between two retainers. The tableau has all the simplicity and power of a medieval woodcut.

There is, moreover, an intimate relationship between the kingship of Jesus that explodes onto Mark's canvas in Chapter 15 and the theme of the kingdom of God that has dominated his Gospel from its beginning. After Jesus has died, the man who buries him, Joseph of Arimathea, is described as one "looking for the kingdom of God" (Mark 15:43). He does not realize that God's kingship has begun to arrive in Jesus' death. And even Psalm 22, whose first, despairing verse Jesus quotes on the cross, ends with a proclamation of God's kingship. In the crucifixion of king Jesus, even in the way in which he sinks to the depths of human despair, the royal power of God is being revealed for those with eyes to see.

This emphasis on the kingship of Jesus in the passion narrative reflects an association between death and God's kingship that is well-nigh universal. The Emily Dickinson poem quoted at the beginning of this chapter makes this connection; the "certain Slant of light" that becomes visible on winter afternoons is termed "An imperial affliction / Sent us of the Air" and compared to "the Distance / On the look of Death." In another Dickinson poem, which is quoted on page 79, the onlookers gathered at the bed of a dying person hold their breaths as they await "that last Onset—when the King / Be witnessed—in the Room."

Why is death a revelation of the kingship of God? Why is it a moment "when the King / Be witnessed— in the Room"? Perhaps because it is something that everyone wishes to prevent, but cannot. No matter what our station in life, no matter how great our wealth, no matter how universal our fame, we cannot stop it. When this master speaks, no one can contradict him; when he decides to enter a room, no one can stop him. Death reveals conclusively that in the last analysis it is God, and not we ourselves, who rules our lives. This is probably at least part of the reason that in the Jewish tradition the Kaddish prayer, which is an acclamation on God's kingship, is chanted by mourners.

But if this were all there was to it, there would be some doubt as to whether God was truly a king or merely a tyrant. Indeed, Elie Wiesel recalls entertaining precisely this doubt upon his arrival at Auschwitz. Someone began reciting the Kaddish, and Wiesel's father joined in. "For the first time, I felt revolt rise up in me. Why should I bless His name? The Eternal, Lord of the Universe, the All-Powerful and Terrible, was silent. What had I to thank Him for?" The most terrible aspect of Wiesel's book *Night* is its description of this loss of faith, not in God's existence, but in his goodness. If God is a despot who rules solely on the basis of force, if he cruelly ignores the suffering of his subjects, can he truly be called a king?

For a true king is not only someone who surpasses others in strength and ability to enforce his will but also someone who outdoes others in active concern for his people's welfare. And this is the dimension of kingship that is emphasized ironically in Mark's passion narrative. "He saved others; himself he cannot save," the mockers say (Mark 15:31), thinking that this gibe invalidates any claim Jesus might have to be "the King of Israel." They do not see the ironic truth in what they say: Jesus *cannot* save himself, *in order that* he might save others; for his mission is to reveal his kingship by giving his life "as a ransom for many" (Mark 10:45). For to be a true king may ultimately mean to take a final step that only a king can take: to give up everything, to abandon every prerogative of rank, every chance of lording it over others, even every chance of saving oneself, in order to benefit the people with whom one has identified oneself.

The ironic truth of the high priests' statement, therefore, suggests that, in the dark events of Good Friday, God was paradoxically intervening for the salvation of humankind. This, of course, is why, in spite of its commemoration of a death, "we call this Friday good." Might there also be some redemptive purpose behind the terrible events of the Holocaust, and behind innocent suffering in general? One is well aware, even in toying with such an idea, of its dangers. One is reminded of the assertion in Dostoevsky, to which we will return later, that if the suffering of just one innocent child were the price God required for the eternal happiness of all of humanity, the price would be too high.

And yet . . . And yet . . . If the innocent do suffer in this world—and they do—isn't it more comforting to believe that their suffering has some higher purpose than to think that it doesn't? If we, as Christians, believe that not a sparrow falls to the ground without it being our heavenly father's will (Matthew 10:29; Luke 12:6), must not there be some redemptive purpose to the millions of innocent men, women, and children falling to the ground?

But such thoughts must not be shouted. They can only be whispered. Perhaps they should not be said at all.

IV

"Father, Forgive Them"

Anne Frank, 1941. © ANNE FRANK-FONDS, BASEL

"This Cruelty Too Will End"

Saturday, July 15, 1944

Dear Kitty,

 . . . "For in its innermost depths youth is lonelier than old age." I read this saying in some book and I've always remembered it, and found it to be true . . . Anyone who claims that the older ones have a more difficult time here, certainly doesn't realize to what extent our problems weigh down on us, problems for which we are probably much too young, but which thrust themselves upon us continually, until, after a long time, we think we've found a solution, but the solution doesn't seem able to resist the facts which reduce it to nothing again. That's the difficulty in these times: ideals, dreams, and cherished hopes rise within us, only to meet the horrible truth and be shattered.

It's really a wonder that I haven't dropped all my ideals, because they seem so absurd and impossible to carry out. Yet I keep them, because in spite of everything I still believe that people are really good at heart. I simply can't build up my hopes on a foundation consisting of confusion, misery, and death. I see the world gradually being turned into a wilderness, I hear the ever approaching thunder, which will destroy us too, I can feel the sufferings of millions and yet, if I look up into the heavens, I think that it will all come right, that this cruelty too will end, and that peace and tranquillity will return again.

In the meantime, I must uphold my ideals, for perhaps the time will come when I shall be able to carry them out.

Yours, Anne

—From *The Diary of Anne Frank*, pp. 218–19

A Reading from the Gospel According to Luke

When they came to the place that is called the Skull, they crucified Jesus there with the criminals, one on his right and one on his left. Then Jesus said, "Father, forgive them; for they do not know what they are doing . . ."

One of the criminals who were hanged there kept deriding him and saying, "Are you not the Messiah? Save yourself and us!" But the other rebuked him, saying, "Do you not fear God, since you are under the same sentence of condemnation? And we indeed have been condemned justly, for we are getting what we deserve for our deeds, but this man has done nothing wrong." Then he said, "Jesus, remember me when you come into your kingdom." He replied, "Truly I tell you, today you will be with me in Paradise." (Luke 23:33–34a, 39–43)

EACH OF THE EVANGELISTS, in telling the story of Jesus' last hours, draws both upon historical memories and upon his own idea of the significance of Jesus.

It is a question not only of who Jesus *was,* but also of who he *is* for the evangelist and his community. So it is not surprising that, in some ways, the different evangelists' pictures of the passion events are different in tone. None of the evangelists, I believe, would think that he was lying, but each is shaping his material to reflect his experience of the one whom he knows not only as a dead hero but also as a living Lord.

So, for example, Luke's picture of Jesus' crucifixion and death emphasizes the theme of forgiveness much more strongly than the other Gospels do. This is also a theme that comes to expression elsewhere in Luke's Gospel; think, for example, of the parable of the prodigal son (Luke 15:11–32) and the story of the sinful woman whom Jesus forgave, "because she loved much" (Luke 7:47). Both of these passages are found only in Luke. So also, here in the passion narrative, Jesus forgives those who crucify him and promises a place in paradise to the repentant criminal who is crucified alongside him.

But besides Luke's own interest in forgiveness, this story may also reflect the ancient Jewish custom of deathbed prayer, in which a request for forgiveness probably played a role. This custom of deathbed prayer continues among religious Jews today, and a form of it, the *vidui,* was on the lips of religious Jews as they marched off to the gas chambers during the Holocaust:

May my death be an atonement for all the sins, iniquities and transgressions of which I have been guilty against thee. Bestow upon me the abounding happiness that is treasured up for the righteous. Make known to me the path of life: in thy presence is fulness of joy; at thy right hand bliss for evermore . . . Into thy hand I commit my spirit; thou hast redeemed me, O Lord God of truth . . . The Lord is king; the Lord was king; the Lord shall be king for ever and ever. Blessed be his name, whose glorious kingdom is for ever and ever.

Note that this deathbed prayer contains a confession of sins, a plea for God's forgiveness, a proclamation of God's kingship, and a citation of Psalm 31:5: "Into your hand I commit my spirit."

Although there is no way of knowing for sure whether or not the ancient Jewish deathbed confession included all of these elements, Luke's version of Jesus' last words shows interesting similarities to, as well as differences from, the modern form of the *vidui.* The most obvious similarity is Jesus' usage of the same psalm verse committing his spirit into the hand of God. Furthermore, the theme of God's kingship, which is prominent in the Jewish prayer, comes to the fore in the words of the repentant criminal, "Remember me when you come into your *kingdom"* (Luke 23:42).

But there are also two significant differences. Jesus

does not confess his sins before dying—presumably because he has, in Luke's eyes, no sins to confess. And instead of asking for forgiveness for himself, he asks it for those who crucify him.

Forgiveness. This characteristic Lukan theme strikes a resounding chord in our hearts today. Forgiveness is one of our most cherished values. Indeed, it often seems to have become our supreme value. But it is a value that becomes debased when we forget its huge price. We think that, just because someone asks for forgiveness, he or she will automatically receive it. How many of us have heard or even said these words in animated discussions with our spouses: "I've *said* I was sorry; what more do you want?" Saying I'm sorry (and of course there were probably extenuating circumstances) makes everything all right. The murderer is sorry about the murder he committed; granted, that won't bring his victim back to life, but he's not to be blamed; at least he's contrite.

The prayer at the commemoration of the liberation of Auschwitz by Elie Wiesel, the Nobel Prize laureate, and a survivor of that camp, combats this debasement of the concept of forgiveness and sharpens our sense of its seriousness. It thus leads us to a deeper understanding of Jesus' prayer, even though on the face of it Wiesel seems to be saying the opposite of Jesus.

Even though we know that God is full of mercies, still we pray to you, O God: do not have pity on those who established this place. God of forgiveness, do not forgive the murderers of Jewish children . . . Those who are here remember the nightly marches [into the gas chambers] of children, and more children, and more children. Frightened, quiet. So quiet and so beautiful. If we could just see one of them our heart would break. But did it break the heart of the murderers? O God, O merciful God, do not have pity on those who did not have mercy on Jewish children.

Who can argue with such a prayer? Is a prayer like his, asking God *not* to forgive the murderers of such children, ethically inferior to Jesus' prayer for his murderers to be forgiven? I hardly think that's the right way to look at it. It's important to distinguish some differences between the two prayers.

For one thing, Jesus asks for forgiveness for his *own* executioners, not for the murderers of little children. And indeed elsewhere, in a passage that Luke along with the other Gospels includes, Jesus warns of the judgment facing those who perpetrate outrages against little ones: it would have been better for them to have a millstone slung around their neck and to be cast into the sea (Luke 17:1–2; Mark 9:42; Matthew 18:6–7).

This is exactly the sort of retribution that Holocaust victims dreamed would one day be visited on their torturers and the murderers of their children. We recall again Moses Schulstein's haunting vision of the shoes of the death-camp victims lining up and marching off with "steps that measure out the judgment." Who would dare to condemn such a vision? Who would dare to question the hope that God will some-day, somehow, right the balances by measuring out his righteous judgment against those who have shot helpless old people and thrown live babies into the fire? As Ivan Karamazov says, "I must have retribution or I shall destroy myself."

And yet, having said this, second thoughts immediately arise. Where exactly is one to draw the line between those who will be forgiven and those who won't be? And who is to draw that line? And how exactly do we know on which side of that line *we* will fall? The lines between the righteous and the unrighteous are not always so clear. On the one hand, the two criminals who are executed with Jesus *have* committed crimes, and the one who turns toward Jesus in repentance admits that his death sentence is a just punishment for what he has done. Luke tactfully refrains from specifying the crimes, but it's a safe bet that they added up to more than a few minor infractions. So we are still left with the offensive idea of wiping clean a dirty slate, or what Paul calls the justification of the ungodly (Romans 4:5). On the other hand, it is a sad fact that those who are abused—physically, sexually, and/or psychologically—often become abusers in their turn. This includes some Holocaust victims, as their children and some of their neighbors may attest. Moral calculus is not always quite so simple as Elie Wiesel's prayer may suggest.

So where does this leave us? On the one hand, it leaves us without grounds for despising or feeling superior to a prayer such as Wiesel's, especially when Our Lord, in his humanity, expressed similar sentiments. We should not be too quick to vault over the human level, or to demand that others do so, in order to land in the lap of the gods.

On the other hand, it makes all the more extraordinary an act of true forgiveness such as is ascribed to Jesus in our passage. Such an act is visible in one of the final entries in Anne Frank's famous diary, which is quoted at the beginning of this chapter. Here, amid apocalyptic images of disintegration and death, this fifteen-year-old Jewish girl, in hiding with her family from the Nazi terror, expresses the extraordinary thought that, in spite of everything, she still believes that people are good at heart. "I simply can't build up my hopes," she says, "on a foundation consisting of confusion, misery, and death." Though she does not use the word "forgiveness" in this passage, that is at least part of what she seems to be talking about. For what is forgiveness but refusing to build upon the foundation of confusion, misery, and death that we see all around and experience as emanating from the human beings who surround us? What is forgiveness but believing against all evidence, and acting on the belief, that people are really good at heart, even when they show themselves manifestly not to be?

Such faith in undeserving human beings cannot really be carried out by an act of the human will, but requires the creative power of God who, as the Jewish liturgy reminds us, is the one who gives life to the dead. Anne Frank's diary entry contains not only images of cosmic death and destruction but also a hint of a hope of apocalyptic renewal. She looks up to the heavens and thinks that, somehow, despite the ever-approaching thunder that is turning the world into a wilderness, despite the death machine that will devour her and her companions and millions of others, somehow, despite all this, "it will all come right." A new world is born when a wrong is forgiven; and only the power that destroys and creates worlds can cause forgiveness to bloom within the wilderness of life here on earth.

To return then, finally, to the point I made at the beginning of this chapter: there is probably a relationship between Jesus' two departures from the pattern of the typical Jewish deathbed prayer. He does not confess his sins, and he prays for forgiveness for his murderers rather than for himself. He *can* pray for his murderers because of his sinlessness, because of his more-than-human status. And other human beings who, either knowingly or unknowingly, follow Jesus, and perform similar extraordinary acts of grace, do so not through their own strength but through the apocalyptic, world-embracing, royal power of the holy God.

V

The Dying of the Light

William Blake, *The Soldiers Casting Lots for Christ's Garments,* 1800. FITZWILLIAM MUSEUM, UNIVERSITY OF CAMBRIDGE

I Heard a Fly Buzz When I Died

I heard a Fly buzz—when I died—
The Stillness in the Room
Was like the Stillness in the Air—
Between the Heaves of Storm—

The Eyes around—had wrung them dry—
And Breaths were gathering firm
For that last Onset—when the King
Be witnessed—in the Room—

I willed my Keepsakes—Signed away
What portions of me be
Assignable—and then it was
There interposed a Fly—

With Blue—uncertain stumbling Buzz—
Between the light—and me—
And then the Windows failed—and then
I could not see to see—

—From Emily Dickinson, *The Complete Poems of Emily Dickinson*, #465

A Reading from the Gospel According to Mark

When it was noon, darkness came over the whole earth until three in the afternoon. At three o'clock Jesus cried out with a loud voice, "Eloi, Eloi, lema sabachthani?" which means, "My God, my God, why have you forsaken me?" When some of the bystanders heard it, they said, "Listen, he is calling for Elijah." And someone ran, filled a sponge with sour wine, put it on a stick, and gave it to him to drink, saying, "Wait, let us see whether Elijah will come to take him down." Then Jesus gave a loud cry and breathed his last. And the curtain of the temple was torn in two, from top to bottom. (Mark 15:33–38)

IN LUKE, as we observed in Chapter 4, the atmosphere surrounding Jesus' death is serene and triumphant: Jesus graciously forgives his crucifiers, sovereignly promises the repentant criminal a place with him in paradise, and then hands back his life-breath to the heavenly Father who bestowed it. In Mark, however, the atmosphere is anything but serene. Jesus

cries out with a loud voice, and instead of uttering
words of reconciliation and faith, he shouts into the
engulfing darkness the words of Psalm 22: "My God,
my God, why have you forsaken me?"

These words, needless to say, have caused problems
for Christian theologians from the beginning of the
Church. If Jesus was the Son of God, indeed even God
himself, as the Church came to believe, how could he
have experienced abandonment by God? Does not this
so-called "cry of dereliction" make a mockery of the
Church's claim that Jesus is the Messiah, the Son of
God?

It is not, therefore, surprising that there have been
numerous attempts to alter the cry of dereliction or to
explain it away. Both Luke and John change it to a
citation from the same *group* of Psalms, but one that
presents a more palatable picture of Jesus. Some scholars try to deal with it by arguing that the cry rests on
a mistranslation from the Aramaic. Others point out
that, while Psalm 22 begins on a note of complaint
about abandonment and suffering, it ends with a triumphant declaration of trust in God's power to save
the sufferer and bring redemption to the ends of the
earth.

These, however, are desperate maneuvers. We must
deal with Mark's text as it stands, not with some hy-
pothetical reconstruction of it. And in Mark itself,
Jesus does not allude to the triumphant end of the
psalm but to the desperate anguish of its beginning—

a connection which seems totally appropriate for a man undergoing the cruel pains of crucifixion.

Indeed, the true meaning of Jesus' last cries in Mark may be, not "better" than it appears to be, but "worse." At his death, Jesus cries out "with a loud voice." Previously in the Gospel, the only beings who have cried out "with a loud voice" are the demons (Mark 1:26; 5:7). The implication, therefore, may be that Jesus' last cry is demonic. So fully has he entered into the human condition that he even shares the lostness of human beings who feel themselves cut off from God and in the grip of inimical, anti-God forces.

Such an interpretation would go along with the overall context of the scene of Jesus' death in Mark. To borrow Dylan Thomas's phrase, Mark describes "the dying of the light." His scene is not just one in which a dying person's vision is darkened, as in Homer's formula, "darkness covered his eyes," or as in the Emily Dickinson poem presented on page 79, which closes with the startlingly effective line, "I could not see to see." The scene in Mark, rather, is one of cosmic darkness. This darkness is said to cover either "the whole land" or "the whole earth." The latter translation is particularly attractive because it enables us to see the scene of Jesus' death as a fulfillment of Old Testament prophecy. Amos, talking about the Day of the Lord, the day upon which God's judgment would fall on sinful humanity, reported God's words as: "On that day . . . I will make the sun go down at noon,

and darken the earth in broad daylight" (Amos 8:9).
Mark's report of darkness over the earth from noon on
is probably to be seen as a fulfillment of this prophecy.

Viewed from this perspective, the day of Jesus' crucifixion is the day of judgment, the day upon which
the anti-God forces will be let loose upon the earth to
kill the old world off and, unwittingly, to bring in the
new one. For there is a secret, hidden player in this
drama of the end of days. He was introduced near the
beginning of the Gospel, where he engaged Jesus in
something like hand-to-hand combat (Mark 1:12–13),
but subsequently he seemed to fade from view. Yet
from time to time hints about his continued presence
and malevolent activity have popped up. Although
rarely mentioned by name, he has been working away
behind the scenes, not resting for a moment, stirring
up opposition to Jesus wherever he can, finally using
his human instruments to drive him to the cross. The
cosmic darkness in the crucifixion scene is the culmi-
nation and concrete expression of this adversary's
never-ending quest for more power, more influence,
more destruction.

As J. Louis Martyn notes, shortly after World War
II and the full revelation of the horrors of the Holocaust, the theologian Emil Brunner, lecturing at an
American college, referred several times to the Devil.
In the question period afterward a student politely,
but with a slight touch of Ivy-League condescension,
asked Brunner why he had used such outmoded, su-

perstitious, unscientific language. "I have referred to the Devil for two reasons," Brunner replied. "First, because I find that he plays a very important role in scripture. And second, because I have seen him."

We, too, have seen him, in the photographs of corpses stacked like firewood at Bergen-Belsen, in Solzhenitsyn's account of torture and murder in the Gulag, in the bloody, disfigured bodies of men, women, and children in Rwanda. We sense his presence in the idiocy of the Nazi racial theories, in the absurdity of Stalin's show trials, in the senselessness of the slaughter in Rwanda. It is as if no rationale were too flimsy, no theory too fallacious or even laughable, to serve as a pretext for killing. As long as a theory can justify hatred and murder, it will be believed. As the poet Michael Deshe wrote after meeting Holocaust survivors:

> Don't condemn man
> His cruelty is his game.
> Don't despise the son of man
> Like a child he loves to play in blood.

This delight in playing in blood sometimes overrules every rational consideration. During the final years of World War II, for example, when the Nazis desperately needed all available trains to supply their troops at the front, they continued to use a significant number of them to deport Jews to the death camps. The imperative of the Final Solution, of advancing the kingdom of death, overrode every other consideration, even the imperative of winning the war. This is why many Jewish leaders in Nazi-occupied Europe were so cruelly deceived—they fondly hoped that, since the Jews were a source of needed manpower, the Nazis would not do anything so irrational as to destroy them. As Leni Yahil has put it in her study of the Holocaust:

> The Nazis were well aware that their "final solution of the Jewish question" was beyond the comprehension of the Jews—or anyone else in the world, for that matter—and that they were operating according to a conception that departed radically from the one common to mankind. Society at large was based on life and strived toward life, and it was incapable of imagining the existence of a counter-society based on, and striving toward, death.

Yet do we not sense a method in this madness—though it is a method that is not human in scope? A method that coolly, rationally, systematically sets out to create as much death as possible? Do we not sense behind it a hidden, ferocious, cunning intelligence? An intelligence that will not rest content until it has broken everything, outraged all innocence, crushed every spirit, consumed all hope, stained and darkened the world with blood?

And so the darkness at Jesus' crucifixion should not

be explained away in some pseudoscientific fashion as the result of an eclipse or a freakish, temporary atmospheric phenomenon. It is the darkness of death, the darkness of the kingdom of Satan, the darkness of the old age of sin and death crushing underneath it the man who had thought to change the course of the world and redirect it into the realms of light. And that man, feeling himself swallowed up by the darkness he had hoped to conquer through God's help, feeling himself cut off from the God who has been his life, cries out in horror at his apparent mistake: "My God, my God: why have you forsaken me?"

And yet, as exegetes from Martin Luther on have pointed out, anyone who cries out to God hopes in God. Anyone who says *"my* God" still hopes against hope, against all evidence, even against all certainty, that God will again show himself to be his God. He still feels himself bound to God, related to him in a special way, part of his family, even if God has for the moment—and maybe even for eternity—hidden his face from him. As Job said, "Though he kill me, yet I will trust in him" (Job 13:15).

As Robert McAffee Brown recounts, Elie Wiesel tells the story of the trial of God that was held at Auschwitz. The judges were three great Talmudic scholars who were inmates in that place. Witnesses were heard, evidence was gathered. The trial went on for several nights. Finally the evidence was complete, and the three judges issued their unanimous verdict:

The Lord God Almighty, Creator of Heaven and Earth, was found *guilty* of crimes against creation and humankind. And then, after what Wiesel describes as "an infinity of silence," the Talmudic scholars looked at the sky and said, "It's time for evening prayers," and the members of the tribunal recited Maariv, the evening service.

"Though he kill me, yet I will trust in him." "Though you have forsaken me, yet you remain my God." This is the faith of the crucified Jesus. This is the victory that overcomes the world.

VI

It Is Finished!

Anna Klausnerová (1932–1944), Theresienstadt,
Passover Seder. JEWISH MUSEUM, PRAGUE

A Hill in Bergen-Belsen

ANNA WAS AMONG the tens of thousands who succumbed to the typhus epidemic in Bergen-Belsen. Her friends gave her up for dead and told her that her struggle with death was useless. But Anna was determined to live. She knew that if she lay down, the end would come soon and she would die like so many others around her. So, in a delirious state, she wandered around the camp, stumbling over the dead and the dying. But her strength gave way. She felt that her feet were refusing to carry her any farther. As she was struggling to get up from the cold, wet ground, she noticed in the distance a hill shrouded in gray mist. Anna felt a strange sensation. Instantly, the hill in the distance became a symbol of life. She knew that if she reached the hill, she would survive, but if she failed, the typhus would triumph.

Anna attempted to walk toward the hill which continually assumed the shape of a mound of earth, a huge grave. But the mound remained Anna's symbol of life, and she was determined to reach it. On her hands and knees, she crawled toward the strange mound of earth that now was the essence of her survival. After long hours passed, Anna reached her destination. With feverish hands she touched the cold mound of earth. With her last drop of strength, she crawled to the top of the mound and collapsed. Tears started to run down her cheeks, real human, warm tears, her first tears since her incarceration in concentration camps some four years ago. She began to call her father. "Please, Papa, come and help me. I know that you, too, are in camp. Please, Papa, help me, for I cannot go on like this any longer."

Suddenly, she felt a warm hand on top of her head. It was her father stroking her just as he used to place his hand over her head every Friday night and bless her. Anna recognized her father's warm, comforting hands. She began to sob even more and told him that she had no strength to live any longer. Her father listened and caressed her head as he used to. He did not recite the customary blessing but, instead, said, "Don't worry, my child. You will manage to survive for a few days, for liberation is very close."

That occurred on Wednesday night, April 11, 1945. On Sunday, April 15, the first British tank entered Bergen-Belsen.

When Anna was well enough to leave the hospital in the British Zone where she was recovering from typhus, she returned to Bergen-Belsen. Only then did she learn that the huge mound of earth in the big square where she spent the fateful night of April 11 in her combat with typhus was a huge mass grave. Among thousands of victims buried beneath the mound of earth was her father, who had perished months earlier in Bergen-Belsen. On that night when she won her battle with death, Anna was weeping on her father's grave.

—From Yaffa Eliach, *Hasidic Tales of the Holocaust,* pp. 177–78

A Reading from the Gospel According to John

Meanwhile, standing near the cross of Jesus were his mother, and his mother's sister, Mary the wife of Clopas, and Mary Magdalene. When Jesus saw his mother and the disciple whom he loved standing beside her, he said to his mother, "Woman, behold your son." Then he said to the disciple, "Behold your mother." And from that hour the disciple took her into his own home.

After this, when Jesus knew that all was now finished, he said (in order to fulfill the scripture), "I am thirsty." A jar full of sour wine was standing there. So they put a sponge full of wine on a branch of hyssop and held it to his mouth. When Jesus had received the wine, he said, "It has been accomplished." Then he bowed his head and gave up his spirit. (John 19:25–30)

IF THE DEATH SCENE in Mark is characterized by an emphasis on Jesus' piercing agony and isolation, and that in Luke is characterized by an emphasis on his compassionate forgiveness, then that in John is characterized by an emphasis on his sovereignty even in death. In John's version of Jesus' last moments, Jesus is concerned, not with his own condition, but with the accomplishment of his mission and with the welfare of those whom he leaves behind.

Like the other evangelists, John emphasizes that Jesus' death on the cross is the fulfillment of scripture. He, however, is very explicit about this, while the other Gospels merely imply it. He tells us explicitly that the soldiers' action of casting lots for Jesus' garments fulfilled the words of Psalm 22, "They parted my garments among them, and for my clothing they cast lots." He adds, *"So* the soldiers did this"—that is, the real reason for their action, though unbeknownst to them, was to fulfill the scripture. When Jesus is about to die, similarly, he says, "I am thirsty," not so much because he really is parched, but, again, in order to fulfill the scripture (John 19:23–25). And, fittingly, Jesus' last words are, "It has been accomplished."

But what exactly is it that Jesus' death accomplishes, according to John? For John, the crucifixion is already, in a sense, Pentecost. Already at the crucifixion the Church is born and empowered with the Spirit. Before he dies, Jesus commits his beloved disciple to his mother's care and his mother to that disciple's care. He says to his mother, "Behold your son!" and to his disciple, "Behold your mother!" That is, from now on the disciple, and the Christian community that he symbolizes, is to continue Jesus' work on earth, is, in a real sense, to *be* Jesus. The Christian community can do this because Jesus, before he dies, hands over his spirit, his life-force. On the one hand, he hands it over to God, from whom he received it. But he also, in a sense, hands it over to his disciples. Even his bowing of his head at the moment of death can be interpreted as a nod in their direction. Out of Jesus' death comes life for his followers.

One of Emily Dickinson's poems speaks of a similar sort of renewal, of life emerging out of death:

> In snow thou comest—
> Thou shalt go with the resuming ground,
> The sweet derision of the crow,
> And Glee's advancing sound.
>
> In fear thou comest—
> Thou shalt go at such a gait of joy
> That man anew embark to live
> Upon the depth of thee.

—From Emily Dickinson, *The Complete Poems of Emily Dickinson,* #1669

Here the unspecified person who is addressed arrives in fear, but will depart—presumably to death—in such a way that others "embark to live" upon his or her depth. We have here, apparently, a prophecy of transformation. The poet looks at a person who lives in the grip of anxiety, but she sees within this person the seed of a new being who will be a source of empowerment not only for that person, but also for those around him or her. In the same way, in Luke's Gospel, shortly before his passion begins, Jesus prophesies both Peter's ignominious abandonment of him and his subsequent transformation into a source of empowerment for others: "But when you have turned again, strengthen your brothers and sisters" (Luke 22:32).

The exact way in which Dickinson describes this transformed person is worth pondering. He or she will be such "That man anew embark to live / Upon the depth of thee." There are people of such depth, such substance, such solidity, that others may, as it were, stand on the firm ground they provide and embark on their own lives through them. This, of course, is the role that all of us who are parents hope to play for our children, though we do so with varying, usually incomplete, success. It is what we, in turn, have looked for from our own parents, and have found to a greater or lesser degree. Or, later in life, we may be lucky enough to find such an embarkation point in a friend, a mentor, a psychotherapist, or even a priest, rabbi, or minister—anything is possible! And what a privilege it is if we ourselves may become the embarkation point for others.

This wonderful process, whereby people become the solid base by means of which others may face the world, went on even amid the horrors of the Holocaust. At the beginning of the present chapter, for

example, one of the children's drawings from Theresienstadt depicts a Passover meal, a seder, in which
about twenty children are seated around a large, care-
fully arranged table. The vision is one of order and
even of grace. The scene is lit by two candles placed
near the master of ceremonies at the head of the table;
their soft glow is reflected in the traditional Passover
plate and in some of the seated figures. And the whole
drawing is reassuringly presided over by a large, confi-
dent-looking adult figure on the upper left, who seems
to constitute the firm anchor for the entire scene—the
embarkation point for those seated around the table.

Yaffa Eliach's story of Anna, the typhus victim from
Bergen-Belsen (pages 91–93), makes a similar point.
Even death does not stop Anna's father from coming
to her, blessing her, promising her that she will live,
and encouraging her to hold on just a little while
longer. Death cannot stop those deep persons in our
lives from becoming embarkation points for us. Indeed, their importance may even grow. We may come
to see aspects of who they were for us that we never
realized while they were alive. To quote another Dickinson poem:

> We learn in the Retreating
> How vast an one
> Was recently among us—
> A Perished Sun

Endear in the departure
How doubly more
Than all the Golden presence
It was—before—

—From Emily Dickinson, *The Complete Poems of
Emily Dickinson,* #1083

A few months ago, while I was on sabbatical leave
in Norway, I received a letter from my mother back in
Chicago. She told me that the mother of a childhood
friend, a woman named Pat Nicholson, who had over
the years become my own good friend, had suddenly
and unexpectedly died. Pat was the sort of woman
upon whose depth many, many people embarked, as
was apparent from my mother's description of her
huge funeral. She was also a big woman physically.
She was expansive in other ways as well: witty, intelli-
gent, a good storyteller, an openhearted friend, and an
active person in the community.

But what I prized most of all about Pat was the
kind of luminous sanity she possessed. During my tur-
bulent adolescence I came to look upon the Nicholson
home as a kind of sanctuary, even though the Nichol-
sons were a big Catholic family with eight children
and usually a kind of cheerful pandemonium reigned
in their smallish, somewhat ramshackle old house. But
just being there, in Pat's presence, somehow seemed to
sort things out for me, to put the pieces back together

again. As one of the characters in Toni Morrison's *Beloved* describes the effect of his lover upon him: "She gather me, man. The pieces I am, she gather them and give them back to me in all the right order."

So it came as a shock to me to hear that Pat Nicholson was dead. And I kept thinking back to a day last December, when I was visiting my parents in Chicago for a few days. Driving past the Nicholson house on my way home from the store, I slowed down, thinking that maybe I'd drop in and have a chat with Pat. But no one seemed to be home, so I drove on, and didn't stop by again. Neither did I phone, thinking that I'd catch Pat on my next trip to America.

But I won't, of course, be able to catch her now. And I wish so much that I had made more of an effort, and that I had stopped by to see her, just for one of those short little half-hour visits where we'd sit around the kitchen table and have a beer together and catch up on each other's lives. Because, if I had, now I would at least have that last conversation to look back on and I could comfort myself with the thought that I had, in a way, said good-bye.

Whenever I visited, Pat would give me a big bearhug at the door when I arrived, and another big bearhug at the door when I left. And if I had made more of an effort, if I had seen her, I would at least have had that last embrace to look back on. But now I don't. And since I don't like to blame *myself* for things, I actually find myself at times being angry with *her* for having gone away so suddenly. The words from an old Leonard Cohen song run through my mind, repeated in a bitter tone: *"Hey! That's* no way to say good-bye!"

I realize the rashness of comparing my sense of loss with regard to Pat Nicholson with that of Holocaust survivors. She, after all, died a natural death; she was not shoved into a gas chamber, or shot in front of my eyes, or killed by starvation and typhus. Still, from a biblical perspective, "natural death" is a misnomer, and there is a sense in which every death is a violation of the God-willed order for creation, as the account in Genesis 1–3 makes clear. Or as the Book of Wisdom puts it: "God created us for incorruption, and made us in the image of his own eternity, but through the devil's envy death entered the world" (2:23–24).

In any event, many Holocaust survivors testify that this is one of their torments—not having had time to say a proper good-bye. Partly because the guards were standing there with whips, screaming at them to keep moving. Partly because the survivors didn't know that they weren't ever going to see their mothers, or fathers, or sisters, or brothers again—because they didn't know that this parting was for eternity.

In the Synoptic Gospels, Jesus' departure from the disciples is this same sort of abrupt, violent leave-taking. He is torn from their midst, and they don't ever get a chance to see him again until he is raised from the dead. But things are different in John's Gospel. Here Jesus *does* get a chance to say good-bye, at least to his mother and one of his male disciples, who are gathered at the foot of his cross. Scholars have argued endlessly about whether this Johannine picture is historical, or whether the picture in the Synoptic Gospels, where they're far away from the cross, is more correct. Or, perhaps, some have suggested, the two pictures can somehow be harmonized—for example by postulating that the onlookers *started out* far away, but *later* moved close up.

I think such harmonizations miss the point. In the Gospels, as in Hasidic stories like that of Anna from Bergen-Belsen, as in many stories that deal with ultimate reality, the line between fact and imagination often becomes thin and blurry. We learn in the retreating how vast a one was among us. Our memories of what the person was like before the "retreat" become suffused with the profound weight of postmortem insight. Perhaps, historically, Jesus died more as he does in Mark than as he does in John. Perhaps he cried out, "My God, why have you forsaken me?" rather than "It has been accomplished." Still, Christians cannot help seeing the story of his death in the context of who they believe him to be, of who they *know* him to be. And they know him to be the one who turns them outward, turns them toward people to whom they are not physically related, identifying these people as their spiritual mothers or fathers or sisters or brothers. And they know that Jesus breaks down the barriers between people and creates this new family by the power that flows from his death for humanity.

I wish I had had a chance to say good-bye to Pat Nicholson. But she was, and is, part of the church to which I also belong, and even if we did not get to say good-bye to each other last December, that is not the end of the story. For Jesus' penultimate words in John contain a promise, not only for this life, but also for the life that stretches beyond it: "Behold, your mother! . . . Behold, your son!"

VII

The Earthquake

The final liquidation of the Warsaw Ghetto, 1943.
YIVO INSTITUTE FOR JEWISH RESEARCH, NEW YORK, N.Y.

The Holy Feat

ACCORDING TO Rabbi Haim of Volozhin, praying for relief from one's own misery is never the ultimate aim of a pious prayer—the prayer of the just. The goal of all prayer remains the need of the Most High for the prayer of the just, in order that he may bring into existence, sanctify, and elevate the worlds. But to the degree that the suffering of each person is already the great suffering of God who suffers for that person, for that suffering that, though "mine," is already his, already divine—the "I" who suffers may pray, and, given God's participation, may pray for himself or herself. One prays for oneself with the intention of suspending the suffering of God, who suffers in my suffering. The self need not pray to mitigate its own suffering: God is already with me, before any asking. Is it not said (in Psalm 91:15): "I am with him in suffering"? And does not Isaiah 63:9 speak of God who suffers in the suffering of man? The suffering self prays to alleviate the "great suffering" of God who suffers, to relieve the suffering of God, who suffers both for man's sin and for the suffering necessary for his atonement. And in that suffering of God which is greater than his own, and toward which, in his prayer, he rises, man's own suffering is assuaged. Man no longer feels his own pain, compared to a torment surpassing his own, in God. Precisely therein lies atonement: in that measure in which God's suffering exceeds my own. It is in God's suffering that the redemption of sin is realized—to the point of abridging suffering. A holy feat: bitterness sweetened by bitterness!

—From Emmanuel Levinas, "Judaism and Kenosis," p. 130

A Reading from the Gospel According to Matthew

At that moment the curtain of the temple was torn in two, from top to bottom. The earth shook, and the rocks were split. The tombs also were opened, and many bodies of the saints who had fallen asleep were raised. After his resurrection they came out of the tombs and entered the holy city and appeared to many. Now when the centurion and those with him, who were keeping watch over Jesus, saw the earthquake and what took place, they were terrified and said, "Truly this man was God's Son!" (Matthew 27:51–54)

I FIRST VISITED Germany in 1987. I was there to attend a New Testament conference in the old university town of Göttingen. This was my first trip to Europe, and I suppose that I played to perfection the role of the innocent abroad, the gawking American out to sample the splendors of the Old World.

On arriving at Göttingen, some friends and I had picked up from the Tourist Information Center a little pamphlet with a self-guided walking tour of the town, and one afternoon we took the tour, observing the architecture of the old city and the other sights to be seen. I noticed that one of the streets was called "Judenstrasse," that is, the Jews' street; this, obviously, was where some of the city's Jews had lived before the Second World War. It gave me a strange feeling to look down that street, which seemed to be haunted by the ghosts of the vanished Jews. In the second-floor window of an apartment facing the street I saw a rather large, hard-faced old woman dressed in an apron looking out. I wondered if her family had taken over the flat when the town's Jews had been deported.

The city authorities of Göttingen have erected a small memorial to the murdered Jews of the city, and the memorial is one of the stops on the walking tour. The inscription on the memorial quotes from one of the psalms of lament, which complains to God about the persecution of Israel:

> All this has come upon us,
> though we have not forgotten you,
> or been false to your covenant . . .
> Because of you we are being killed all day long,
> and accounted as sheep for the slaughter.
> (Psalm 44:17, 22)

Somehow, I felt myself drawn to this memorial, and I wanted to spend a few more minutes there. My friends, however, wanted to move on—there were several more stops on the walking tour, and it was getting near to dinnertime. I was tempted to say that I'd stay for a little while and meet them later. But I didn't. We moved off, and the only comment anyone made was, "Well, it's nice that the Germans have put these things up—you see them all over the country."

The next day I felt a powerful urge to go back to the memorial. It was as though I had a rendezvous that had to be kept. In the afternoon I returned by myself, read the inscription again, and suddenly felt an upheaval within myself—almost like an earthquake. I sat down on a bench and began to cry. People walked by on the nearby street, seemingly oblivious. Perhaps my weeping was inaudible and invisible from the distance. Or perhaps it was not so unusual to see someone weeping by this memorial. But I remember one young woman glancing at me as she passed by, seeming to hesitate for a moment, and then walking on. I wished, and I wish now, that she had stopped, though I don't know what I would have said to her, or what she could have said to me.

And I remember thinking: how can people just go about their daily business as if nothing had happened here? How can life go on as normal in a place where the ground is so soaked with blood, where there are so many ghosts of murdered men, women, and children floating around? Why doesn't the earth open its mouth and swallow this place up?

In Matthew's Gospel, Jesus' death *is* followed by an

earthquake. Not only is the curtain of the Temple torn, as in the other Synoptic Gospels, but there is also an earthquake, the rocks are split, and many bodies of holy people come out of the tombs and go into Jerusalem, where they are seen by many.

Similar prodigies were often connected with the deaths of the great in antiquity. Virgil, for example, describes how, at the murder of Julius Caesar, the sun hid itself, Mount Etna poured forth molten rock, the Alps quaked, and pale ghosts were seen in the night (*Georgics,* 1.463–90). It is difficult to know whether or not Virgil means these descriptions to be taken literally. In any case, there is a symbolic point to them: the murder of Caesar was an act of literally earthshaking horror. The outrage of it was so great that it upset the balance of nature. This seems to be part of what Matthew is trying to get across with his description of the supernatural happenings that followed Jesus' death: even nature registered the cosmic horror of that outrage.

But, in the biblical context in which Matthew's Gospel is written, there is more to it than that. Darkness on the earth; earthquakes; God's judgment poured out on his holy Temple; the resurrection of the dead. These were events that were expected to happen at the end of time, when God would bring the dominion of Satan to an end and inaugurate his own dominion of righteousness and peace on the earth. By picturing such events as occurring at Jesus' death, Matthew is saying that already in that death a victory over Satan was won and the new age had broken in. The moment of Jesus' death, then, was not only a moment of destruction but also a moment of revelation. It is therefore fitting that the centurion and the other soldiers, seeing those events, should gain a sudden insight into Jesus' identity, which is the key to the new age: "Truly, this man was the Son of God!"

This interpretation, however, immediately raises theological questions—questions with which we have been struggling throughout this book. If the earth quaked at Jesus' death, why did it not tremble at the death of six million of his fellow-Jews? If, in the Old Testament, it opened up to swallow Korah, Dathan, and Abiram for offering strange fire on the altar of the Lord (Numbers 16), why did it not open up to swallow Hitler, Eichmann, and Himmler for creating at Auschwitz a strange fire whose flames leaped up to heaven? And if Jesus' death meant the defeat of Satan, why does Satan, to quote the title of a popular book of the late 1970s, still seem to be alive and well and living on planet Earth—even now, fifty years after the Holocaust, and over nineteen hundred and fifty years after Jesus' death?

Somehow, if one believes in God, one believes that there must be an answer to such questions. But do such affirmations of faith in divine providence really help? Do they ultimately make any difference at all?

In one of her most brilliant poems, Emily Dickinson seems to question whether they do:

> I reason, Earth is short—
> And Anguish—absolute—
> And many hurt,
> But, what of that?
>
> I reason, we could die—
> The best Vitality
> Cannot excel Decay,
> But, what of that?
>
> I reason, that in Heaven—
> Somehow, it will be even—
> Some new Equation, given—
> But, what of that?

—From Emily Dickinson, *The Complete Poems of Emily Dickinson*, #301

The first two stanzas propound a sort of stoic resignation in the face of decay, suffering, and death. Yes, such defects in the universe exist, and there is no way of preventing them—but what of that? Then, in the third stanza, Dickinson echoes the religious person's hope that somehow, in heaven, the balance of suffering will be righted—only to cut the ground out from under the relevance of this hope with a final, devastating repetition of, "But, what of that?" Yes, in heaven all tears may be wiped away, all suffering may be compensated for by some "new Equation"—but does that really make any difference to the person who is suffering *now?*

One of the most haunting images of the Holocaust is a photograph taken by a German army photographer during the final liquidation of the Warsaw Ghetto, in the spring of 1943 (page 106). As David Roskies points out, in the background one can see German soldiers who are rounding up Jewish men, women, and children for deportation to Auschwitz. The victims face every which way, but none of them seems to be looking at the others. All of them have their hands in the air. Separated from the rest by a small space is a young boy who looks to be seven or eight years old. He is neatly dressed in shorts, an overcoat, and a cap. Like the others, he has his hands in the air. But he seems to be with no one, separated even from his fellow deportees, and his face, which is physically very beautiful, wears an expression of fear and bewilderment. The soldier behind him is pointing his rifle in the boy's general direction, though apparently not directly at him.

As Roskies notes, the force of the image rests partly in our near-certainty that all the people pictured are doomed, partly in the ludicrous contrast between the boy's smallness and helplessness, on the one hand, and the massive power represented by the soldiers' battle helmets, uniforms, and guns, on the other. The awkward, childish way in which the boy holds his hands in the air is particularly poignant. The gesture of raising one's hands in the air is appropriate to an enemy soldier who has just been disarmed or to a dangerous criminal who has just been apprehended, not to a young child who has done nothing. It is no wonder that this photograph has become the supreme icon of the catastrophe of the Holocaust for people as diverse as Ingmar Bergman and Menachem Begin. It is a beautiful image, and an intensely disturbing one.

This graphic image of violated innocence merges in the mind with verbal images of suffering children described by Ivan Karamazov in Dostoyevsky's great novel *The Brothers Karamazov*. In conversation with his saintly brother Alyosha, a devout Christian, Ivan brings up precisely the suffering of children as the critical challenge to the Christian gospel. With an intensity bordering on obsession, he describes to Alyosha cases of abuse and murder of children he has culled from the newspapers. For example, the five-year-old girl whose parents beat her horribly, smeared her with excrement, locked her in a privy all night in the middle of winter, and left her to die:

> And that mother could sleep at night, hearing the groans of the poor child locked up in that vile place! Do you realize what it means when a little creature like that, who's quite unable to understand what is happening to her, beats her little

aching chest in that vile place, in the dark and cold, with her tiny fist and weeps searing, unresentful and gentle tears to "dear, kind God" to protect her?

Ivan also describes in detail the case of the eight-year-old peasant boy who inadvertently hurt the paw of a rich landowner's dog and was, at the landowner's command, stripped naked, told to run, and then torn apart before his mother's eyes by the landowner's hunting dogs. What do such cases say about the nature of a God who allows them to transpire?

Yet, Ivan protests, he is not an atheist. He wants to believe, but these cases of children's suffering thwart him:

> I want to see with my own eyes the lion lie down with the lamb and the murdered man rise up and embrace his murderer. I want to be there when everyone suddenly finds out what it has all been for. All religions on earth are based on this desire, and I am a believer. But then there are the children, and what am I to do with them? That is the question I cannot answer.

What, indeed, is Ivan to do with the children? It is not that he is unaware of the biblical notion that there will in the end be a final rectification of all earthly wrongs, including the suffering of children. It is not that he is unaware of the idea that in heaven, to apply

Emily Dickinson's words, "Somehow, it will be even— / Some new Equation, given." It is just that for Ivan, as for Dickinson, the "somehow" in that sentence poses an insoluble conundrum. He cannot imagine how that "somehow" could be actualized, how such a divine balancing act could possibly occur:

Oh, Alyosha, I'm not blaspheming! I understand, of course, what a cataclysm of the universe it will be when everything in heaven and on earth blends in one hymn of praise and everything that lives and has lived cries out: "Thou art just, O Lord, for thy ways are revealed!" Then, indeed, the mother will embrace the torturer who had her child torn to pieces by his dogs, and all three will cry aloud, "Thou art just, O Lord!", and then, of course, the crown of knowledge will have been attained and everything will be explained. But there's the rub: for it is that I cannot accept . . . It is not worth one little tear of that tortured little girl who beat herself on the breast and prayed to her "dear, kind Lord" in the stinking privy with her unexpiated tears! It is not worth it, because her tears remain unexpiated . . . And, finally, I do not want a mother to embrace the torturer who had her child torn to pieces by the dogs! She has no right to forgive him! If she likes, she can forgive him for herself, she can forgive the torturer for the immeasurable suffering he has inflicted upon her as a mother; but she has no right to forgive him for the sufferings of her tortured child.

In the dramatic climax of the chapter, Ivan sums up in the sharpest possible way the theological challenge posed by the innocent suffering he has been describing. He turns to the devout Alyosha with the question:

"Tell me frankly, I appeal to you—answer me: imagine that it is you yourself who are erecting the edifice of human destiny with the aim of making men happy in the end, of giving them peace and contentment at last, but that to do that it is absolutely necessary, and indeed quite inevitable, to torture to death only one tiny creature, the little girl who beat her breast with her little fist, and to found the edifice on her unavenged tears—would you consent to be the architect on those conditions? Tell me and do not lie!"

"No, I wouldn't," Alyosha said softly.

Not even the salvation of the whole universe, Ivan asserts—and Alyosha seems to agree—is worth the suffering of one innocent child. The exchange suggests that the answer to the question propounded in the Book of Job, "Can mortal man be more righteous than God?" (Job 4:17), may, terribly enough, be "Yes." If human beings of good will had been given a free hand to design the universe, they might have done a better job than God has. They might at least have taken care to create a world in which innocent children did not have to suffer.

The problem posed to theology by the suffering of innocent children, of course, was not invented by Dostoyevsky. Indeed, it is posed in a way by Matthew's Gospel itself. In Matthew's account of the birth of Jesus, the megalomaniac King Herod, alerted by the wise men and the scriptures about the birth of a new king in Bethlehem, and alarmed by the thought of a potential rival, orders that all children two years of age and younger from the Bethlehem region should be slaughtered. Luckily for Jesus, his father is warned by an angel in a dream and flees to Egypt with his family, where they stay until Herod's death. Unluckily for the children of Bethlehem, no angel warns *their* fathers, and every child dies. All this happened, Matthew tells us, in fulfillment of what had been spoken through the prophet Jeremiah:

> A voice was heard in Ramah,
>   wailing and loud lamentation,
> Rachel weeping for her children;
>   and she refused to be consoled,
>   because they were no more.
>   (Matthew 2:18, citing Jeremiah 31:15)

Not only *The Brothers Karamazov,* then, but also the Gospel of Matthew reverberates with the torment of those who cannot be comforted concerning the death of innocent children. Like Ivan Karamazov, "Rachel," the symbol of the mothers of Bethlehem, refuses to be consoled for the death of her children. For whatever could make up for such a loss? In Ivan's words, how could the tears and moans of all those dying babies ever be expiated? In connection with this question of compensation, is it not almost ludicrous when, at the end of the Book of Job, God restores the happiness and prosperity of Job by giving him ten new children to replace the ten children who had been killed in a single day? As if that would really make up for it!

Even more disturbing than Matthew's description of the slaughter of the innocent children itself is the implication of divine complicity in the event. The "Rachel weeping" passage in Jeremiah 31 implies that God, through his prophet, foresaw and foretold this event. But if he foresaw it, he must also, in a sense, have willed it, as he willed the escape of Jesus. At the very least he did nothing to prevent it. Moreover, Herod is actually warned by the scripture, as interpreted by the chief priests and scribes, about the location of the new king's birth: he is to come from Bethlehem, the city of David, as the prophet Micah had predicted (Matthew 2:4–6, citing Micah 5:2). Thus the scripture, which is God's word, makes an indispensable contribution to the murder of the infants of Bethlehem by informing the king of his enemy's address. This would not be so damning if God, the ultimate author of the scriptures, were not presumed to foresee the effect of his prophetic word. But since he, who "declares the end from the beginning" (Isaiah 46:10), must be supposed to know what will happen, he is at least indirectly implicated. For he has planted in the Bible passage a hint which he must be aware will be used by Herod to ferret out the location of the Messiah's birth. This knowledge, he must surely know, will lead to the murder of the Bethlehem infants—also in fulfillment of his word. The logic is inescapable: God *must* have planned these events from the beginning.

But is *any* event, even the birth of the Messiah, worth such a terrible price? Does not the story turn God himself into the most selfish and callous sort of parent, apprehensive only about the safety of his own Son, blithely unconcerned about the murder of hundreds of other infants? And does it not make Jesus, if not an accomplice in or a beneficiary of murder, at least a survivor burdened with a guilt similar to that of Holocaust survivors—someone who was lucky enough to be saved, while so many others were unlucky enough to be killed?

These are, indeed, unanswerable questions. Unanswerable, at least, so long as one assumes that God, Jesus, and the slaughtered innocents are completely separate beings. But this does not seem to be the way that the Bible would have us view them. Jesus, after all, ends up unjustly murdered, like the babies of Bethlehem, and Matthew's narrative suggests a certain parallelism, perhaps even a mystical identification, between these two outrages. As "Rachel" weeps at the slaughter of her children in Bethlehem, so God himself seems to mourn at the death of Jesus, ripping the curtain of the Temple from top to bottom as human mourners rip their clothes in a gesture of grief. God himself, then, seems to suffer in the death of the innocent Jesus.

Nor is this idea of divine solidarity in suffering an exclusively Christian idea, as the quotation from the Jewish philosopher Emmanuel Levinas at the beginning of this chapter makes clear. In the article from which the quotation is taken, Levinas discusses the linked concepts of divine suffering and prayer in the thought of Haim of Volozhin, a Lithuanian rabbi who lived in the late eighteenth and early nineteenth centuries. These concepts are related to Rabbi Haim's kabbalistic notion that God actually needs humanity for the great task of *tikkun,* of repairing the torn and broken universe. According to Rabbi Haim, one ought to pray not so much to alleviate one's own suffering as to alleviate the immensely greater suffering of God, who suffers in one's own and in all human misery, and in the general brokenness of the world. But in the rising into God's suffering that occurs in prayer, the human subject finds his or her own suffering assuaged in the divine suffering that is so much greater, so that one's own suffering becomes a "bitterness sweetened by bitterness."

The final phrase could well stand as the rubric over

the Gospel passion narratives. Bitterness sweetened by bitterness; human suffering assuaged and transfigured by being taken up into the suffering of God. Jesus' suffering is not his suffering alone, but that of all humanity; and it is also the suffering of God. But this shared suffering is not the final word either. Ultimate reality, rather, somehow embraces and knits together the pain and horror of the crucifixion with the triumph of the resurrection. Indeed, our story speaks of the crucifixion as, already, in some way, a resurrection—the tombs are opened and the dead are raised precisely at Jesus' death, not three days later. This would seem to imply that there is a divine presence and power active in the suffering and death of the innocent, and that somehow this divine power defeats the dominion of death to redeem the world.

And this idea of a divine solidarity and redemptive power in human suffering brings us back to Ivan Karamazov's question, "What am I to do with the children?" For there is a significant difference between the God of Ivan and the God of his brother Alyosha. Ivan is an intellectual; he builds a case against God from the evidence he culls from the newspapers, and the God he longs for is one who will act equitably and rationally in rewarding the good and punishing the bad. Alyosha's vision of God, on the other hand, is centered in the incarnation of Jesus. Although he agrees with Ivan in theoretically rejecting an edifice of salvation founded on the torture of a single innocent child, he goes on to link all innocent suffering with the suffering of Christ, the God-made-man:

> "Ivan," Alyosha said suddenly with flashing eyes, "you said just now, is there a being in the whole world who could or had the right to forgive? But there is such a being, and he can forgive everything, everyone and everything and *for everything,* because he gave his innocent blood for all and for everything. You've forgotten him, but it is on him that the edifice is founded, and it is to him that they will cry aloud: 'Thou art just, O Lord, for thy ways are revealed!' "

And Alyosha himself, in correspondence to his belief in a God incarnate in Christ, is a person who is intensely involved in the world. In contrast to Ivan, he does not occupy his time with cutting out and anthologizing newspaper articles about child abuse but with helping actual children, a group of local village boys. The novel, indeed, ends with some of these boys cheering, "Hurrah for Karamazov!" At least part of Dostoyevsky's answer to Ivan's question, "What am I to do with the children?" is to be found in this picture of the redemptive effect of Alyosha's love.

And what exactly does all this have to do with the Jewish boy with his hands raised into the air, who seems so alone, so helpless, so beautiful in the German military photographer's picture? How was the incarnational God present for him in the midst of all that terror? Where was his Alyosha? I don't know! All I know is that the mystery of this child's suffering must somehow be wrapped up in that other mystery of God's own suffering in the suffering of his Son. Whose innocence was also violated. Who was also separated from his people. Who also proved to be no match for the brutality of the state. Who also lifted up his hands—who "stretched out his arms of love on the hard wood of the cross, that everyone might come within the reach of his saving embrace."

Final Thoughts

Old Jewish Cemetery in Prague. RICHARD NEBESKÝ

The Gravestones in the Old Jewish Cemetery in Prague

Even in death they jostle each other, gesticulate,
Throw furtive glances skyward or bend toward the
   ground.
Uncertain of footing, they lurch to one side,
Nod their heads at a neighbor's remark,
Or lean back in disbelief.
Some of them, certainly, seem to be praying,
Filled with a holy joy but dignified, swaying;
Others seem somewhat tipsy or completely drunk;
A few have been laid low, and can't get up.

Perhaps what agitates them so
Is the bodies beneath their feet,
Jumbled together twelve deep,
And the ghosts that crowd the synagogue behind
   them
Whose flesh and bones have been burned
And can only whisper their names.

The living drift by and from time to time
One of them places a small rock gingerly on a
   gravestone

As if that contact of like against like
Could awaken this one to distant relations
Or convey to that one that life
Continues outside these walls.
Some set a handwritten note beneath their rock
To try to make their message clear.
But the gravestones seem not to hear, or cannot be
bothered;
They are leaning not into the future but into the
past:
Into the past, into a wind
That roars down on them from Sinai.

—Joel Marcus

THE SUMMER after preaching the preceding sermons, I went to Prague for a scholarly conference. Still much in my mind was something I had read shortly before: the transcript of a dialogue concerning "Church, State, People, and Judaism" that took place in Germany in January 1933 between Karl Ludwig Schmidt, a New Testament scholar and Christian theologian, and Martin Buber, an Old Testament scholar, chronicler of Hasidism, and Jewish theologian.

This dialogue was carried out in an atmosphere of frankness, understanding, and great mutual respect. Schmidt was an outspoken member of the "Confessing Church," which opposed the Nazi attempt to take over the German churches and German cultural life in general. In the dialogue itself, he openly repudiates anti-Semitism and attacks Nazism—something that was already becoming an act of courage on January 14, 1933, a little over two weeks before Hitler's accession to power. Because of the danger in which his anti-Nazi stance placed him, Schmidt was forced to leave

Germany for Switzerland two years later, in 1935. Buber, similarly, was a great bridge figure between German Jews and German Christians, both before and after his own exile from Germany in 1938. His works were studied and acclaimed by Christian theologians such as Emil Brunner, and he occupied himself frequently with the question of the relationship between Israel and the Church, writing in later years that he looked upon Jesus as "my great brother."

Two passages from Buber's contributions to the dialogue especially stuck in my mind as I traveled to Prague. The first affirms that, in spite of Israel's knowledge that it has sinned a thousand times against God, it also knows that it has not been rejected by him: "In this discipline and chastisement the hand of God holds us and does not let us go; in this fire it grasps us and does not allow us to fall." Less than ten years later these prophetic words were fulfilled in a more literal manner than Buber himself could imagine in 1933, as millions of Jewish bodies were consumed in the crematoria of Auschwitz, Majdanek, and the other death camps. Buber's unwitting prophecy is a singularly terrible demonstration of the truth of Emmanuel Levinas's adage that "the literal meaning leads further than the metaphor."

The second passage refers more directly to the relation between the church and the synagogue. Buber describes how, from time to time, he returns to the German city of Worms, where his family has ancient roots. Besides being a center of German Judaism, Worms has also been an important city in Christian history; in the sixteenth century, for example, a famous synod was held there at which the Roman Catholic Church for the first time anathematized Martin Luther. There is a beautiful cathedral in Worms, and Buber says that, whenever he goes to the city, he first visits the cathedral and is enthralled by its majestic harmony, in which no part is out of place. He wanders through its splendid interior, gazing at it in perfect joy. He then goes to the Jewish graveyard:

> It consists of cracked and crooked stones without shape or direction. I enter the cemetery and look up from this disorder to the marvelous harmony of the cathedral, and it seems to me as if I were looking from Israel up to the Church. Here below there is no suggestion of form, only the stones and the ashes beneath the stones . . . The corporeality of human beings who have become ashes is there. It is there. It is there for me. It is there for me, not as corporeality within the space of this planet, but as corporeality deep in my own memories, back into the depths of history, back as far as Sinai.
>
> I have stood there; I have been united with the ashes and through them with the patriarchs. That is a remembrance of the divine-human encounter which is granted to all Jews. The perfection of the Christian God-space cannot divert me from this; nothing can divert me from the God-time of Israel.

I have stood there and I have experienced everything myself. I have experienced all the death that
was before me; all the ashes, all the desolation, and
all the noiseless wailings became mine. But the
covenant has not been withdrawn from me. I lie on
the ground, prostrate like these stones. But it has
not been withdrawn from me.

A few months after reading this passage, I found
myself in another Jewish graveyard in Europe, the old
Jewish cemetery in Prague, on the morning of my
departure from that ancient city. This cemetery was
established in the fifteenth century. It quickly ran out
of space, and since the authorities would not allow it
to be expanded, the bodies of Prague's Jews had to be
buried on top of each other, up to twelve deep. The
last burial took place in 1787.

The Jewish graveyard in Prague, like the graveyard
in Worms described by Buber, is made up of a dense
crowd of stones leaning crazily in different directions,
all of them at least two centuries old (see the photograph on page 128). As I wandered through it, the
stones seemed almost human, as old, weather-beaten
gravestones sometimes do, and in my imagination
their varying postures seemed to reflect different human responses to the chaotic storm that had swept
over the Jews of Europe for the past thousand years.
This impression of the gravestones as a crowd battered
by the storm of history was made more forceful by the

fact that entrance to the cemetery is through the Pinchas Synagogue, inside of which the names of over seventy-seven thousand Czech Jews murdered during the Holocaust are inscribed on wall after wall.

Unlike Buber in Worms, I do not recall seeing a church from the Prague Jewish graveyard; the tallest building in the immediate vicinity is the clock tower of the old Jewish city hall. The clock on this tower fascinated one of Prague's most famous citizens, the writer Franz Kafka, who was Jewish himself, from his childhood onward. The hours are marked by Hebrew letters and the hands run "counterclockwise," reflecting the fact that Hebrew reads from right to left. Somehow the backward-running clock fits the backward-looking atmosphere of the old Jewish quarter in general and of the graveyard in particular. Both speak eloquently of a vanished Jewish past.

As I wandered past the tottering gravestones, this sense of contact with the past became palpable, and I felt that in a certain sense my experience was recapitulating Buber's. I was bound up with the crazy disorder of the decaying stones in a way that I had not felt tied to the harmony of the magnificent churches I had visited in Prague. I sensed a continuity, an unbroken chain of Jewish existence that reached all the way back to Sinai. And I saw myself as part of that chain.

But I also experienced another sort of communion as I wandered through the graveyard on the morning of my departure from Prague. A friend was at my side, a good Gentile Christian friend, a sort of respected elder brother in the faith, to adopt and adapt Buber's phrase. And this Christian friend was also responding powerfully to the atmosphere of the graveyard. And he and I shared, and still share, a knowledge of our communion in another and, to us, central facet of the brokenness of the world—the body of Jesus that was broken on the cross. And, to alter Buber's other words, nothing can wrench me away from that communion, either; nothing can remove from me my sense of belonging to, participating in, and being the beneficiary of God's saving encounter with Israel and with the broken world, which occurred in the crucifixion of Jesus.

It is the central intuition of this book that these two forms of communion—with the tragedies of Jewish history, culminating in the Holocaust, and with Jesus' death on the cross—are inextricably bound up with each other. A corollary is that the *tikkun* of the world, its repair, restoration, and redemption—including the redemption of Israel—has already been decisively inaugurated in Jesus' resurrection from the dead. But that corollary belongs essentially to the preaching of Easter rather than to that of Good Friday.

Notes

Preface

On the death of Jesus in the Gospel passion narratives, see Raymond E. Brown, *The Death of the Messiah* (2 vols.; Anchor Bible Reference Library; New York: Doubleday, 1994). Many of the details of my exegesis of the New Testament texts are dependent on Brown's magisterial work. John Dominic Crossan has criticized Brown for attributing too much historicity to the Gospels' emphasis on the involvement of Jews in Jesus' death *(Who Killed Jesus? Exposing the Roots of Anti-Semitism in the Gospel Story of the Death of Jesus* [San Francisco: Harper, 1995]); Brown has responded in a measured way in "The Narratives of Jesus' Passion and Anti-Judaism," *America* 172 (1995) 8–12. On the Holocaust generally, see Lucy S. Dawidowicz, *The War Against the Jews 1933–1945* (New York: Henry Holt and Co., 1975; repr. New York: Bantam Books, 1986); Martin Gilbert, *The Holocaust: A History of the Jews of Europe During the Second World War* (New York: Holt, Rinehart and Winston, 1985); Leni Yahil, *The Holocaust: The Fate of European Jewry* (New York: Oxford University Press, 1990); and the superb publication of the United States Holocaust Memorial Museum, *The World Must Know: The History of the Holocaust as Told in the United States Holocaust Memorial Museum* (Boston: Little, Brown and Company, 1993).

Chapter I: The Suffering Servant

The story about the Lithuanian Jewish youth who pretended to be Jesus is from Yaffa Eliach, *Hasidic Tales of the Holocaust* (New York: Oxford University Press, 1982). On the history of Jewish interpretation of Isaiah 53, see Samuel R. Driver and A. Neubauer, *The Fifty-third Chapter of Isaiah According to the Jewish Interpreters* (2 vols.; Oxford and London: J. Parker, 1876–1877). On disputations between Jews and Christians about the interpretation of biblical texts, see Haim Maccoby, ed., *Judaism on Trial: Jewish-Christian Disputations in the Middle Ages* (London: Littman Library of Jewish Civilization, 1982). On modern scholarly interpretations of Isaiah 53, see H. H. Rowley, *The Servant of the Lord* (Oxford: Basil Blackwell, 1952) 1–93. On modern Jewish attitudes toward Jesus, see Donald A. Hagner, *The Jewish Reclamation of Jesus: An Analysis and Critique of Modern Jewish Study of Jesus* (Grand Rapids: Zondervan, 1984) and Fritz A. Rothschild, ed., *Jewish Perspectives on Christianity* (New York: Crossroad, 1990). The novel by Chaim Potok about the Orthodox Jewish artist who paints crucifixions is *My Name Is Asher Lev* (Greenwich, Conn.: Fawcett Publications, 1972). Martin Buber's views on Jesus are well summed up by Ekkehard W. Stegemann in Rothschild's book, and Vermes's two main books on Jesus are *Jesus the Jew: A Historian's Reading of the Gospels* (Philadelphia: Fortress, 1973) and *The Religion of Jesus the Jew* (London: SCM, 1993). On Chagall's crucifixion scenes, see David G. Roskies, *Against the Apocalypse: Responses to Catastrophe in Modern Jewish Culture* (Cambridge, Mass., and London: Harvard University Press, 1984) 284–89.

Chapter II: "You Are Being Dehumanized"

The story from which the present chapter gets its title is from *The World Must Know,* p. 147 (see notes to Preface). The poem "Isaac," by Amir Gilboa, translated by T. Carmi, is from *The*

Penguin Book of Hebrew Verse (New York: Penguin Books Ltd., 1981), p. 560. The poem "I Saw a Mountain," by Moses Schulstein, translated by Mindele Wajsman and Bea Stadtler, is from *The World Must Know,* pp. 145–47. The essay contrasting the understatement of biblical narrative with the *Odyssey*'s delight in detail is Erich Auerbach, "Odysseus' Scar," in *Mimesis: The Representation of Reality in Western Literature* (Princeton: Princeton University Press, 1953) 3–23. The importance of gaps in biblical narrative is also emphasized by Meir Sternberg, *The Poetics of Biblical Narrative* (Bloomington: Indiana University Press, 1985). Lew Wallace's novel *Ben-Hur: A Tale of the Christ* was first published in 1880, and has been reprinted many times since. There is an account of the controversy over the picture of the naked female prisoners at Yad Vashem in *Hadoar* from February 17, 1995, p. 7. Alexander Solzhenitsyn describes the Soviet "sewage disposal system" in his great record *The Gulag Archipelago* (Glasgow: William Collins & Son, 1974), which is marred only by a tendency to deemphasize Nazi atrocities in comparison to Soviet ones. Emmanuel Levinas's statement about the literal meaning leading further than metaphor appears in *In the Time of the Nations* (Bloomington and Indianapolis: Indiana University Press, 1994) 128.

Chapter III: An Atheist in Five Minutes

The Complete Poems of Emily Dickinson, edited by Thomas H. Johnson, was published by Little, Brown and Company of Boston and Toronto (1970). I have given the version of the Mourner's Kaddish from Philip Birnbaum, ed., *Daily Prayer Book: Sephardic* (New York: Hebrew Publishing Company, 1969) 160. I heard the story about the man who became an atheist in five minutes from C. Fitzsimmons Allison, the former rector of Grace Episcopal Church in New York City. On the use of the Old Testament in the Gospel passion narratives, see Joel Marcus, "The Old Testament and the Death of Jesus: The Role of Scripture in the Gospel Passion Narratives," in John T. Carroll and Joel B. Green, eds., *The Death of Jesus in Early Christianity* (Peabody, Mass.: Hendrickson, 1995) 205–34. On Markan irony, see Jerry Camery-Hoggatt, *Irony in Mark's Gospel* (Cambridge: Cambridge University Press, 1992). On the theme of the kingship of Jesus in Mark's passion narrative, see Donald Juel, *Messiah and Temple: The Trial of Jesus in the Gospel of Mark* (Society of Biblical Literature Dissertation Series 31; Missoula: Scholars Press, 1973) and Frank Matera, *The Kingship of Jesus: Composition and Theology in Mark 15* (Society of Biblical Literature Dissertation Series 66; Chico, Calif.: Scholars Press, 1982). Elie Wiesel tells the story about hearing the Mourner's Kaddish in *Night* (New York: Penguin Books, 1981; orig. 1958) 44–45. "We call this Friday good" is from T. S. Eliot's "East Coker" *(Four Quartets* [San Diego, New York, London: Harcourt Brace Jovanovich, 1971; orig. 1943] 30). Eliot's anti-Semitism has recently been widely publicized; see Anthony Julius, *T. S. Eliot, Anti-Semitism, and Literary Form* (Cambridge: Cambridge University Press, 1995).

Chapter IV: "Father, Forgive Them"

The quotation from Anne Frank is from her diary entry of July 15, 1944 *(The Diary of Anne Frank: The Critical Edition* [New York: Doubleday, 1986]); three weeks later, on August 4, the Nazis burst into the Franks' hiding place, arrested them and the other Jews who were staying with them, and shipped them all to Auschwitz. Only Anne's father survived the war. Many ancient manuscripts do not contain the crucial part of Luke 23:34, in which Jesus prays for God to forgive his crucifiers, but Raymond E. Brown after a long discussion concludes that they were probably a part of the original text *(Death* [see note to preface], 2.975–

81). On Jewish deathbed confession, see Abraham Millgram, *Jewish Worship* (Philadelphia: Jewish Publication Society, 1971) 331. That there was a practice of deathbed confession already in antiquity is indicated by the Mishnah, Tractate Sanhedrin 6:2, and by the Talmud, Tractate Sanhedrin 32a; it may already be reflected in such passages as 2 Maccabees 7:18, 32–33. I have quoted the text of the *vidui* from Joseph H. Hertz, *The Authorized Daily Prayer Book: Revised Edition* (New York: Bloch Publishing Company, 1948) 1065. According to Hertz, this form of the prayer is largely from the medieval Shulchan Aruch, and "embodies the traditional phrases in use since Nachmanides (1194–1270)." It is anybody's guess whether these phrases were in use before the time of Nachmanides, but confession and petition for forgiveness must have been part of such prayers, an association between death and God's kingship is confirmed by the Kaddish, and Psalm 31:5 is a logical biblical verse to repeat on one's deathbed. I have translated Elie Wiesel's Auschwitz prayer from the Hebrew version of it reported in *Hadoar,* February 3, 1995, p. 3. Ivan Karamazov's remark about his longing for retribution is from Fyodor Dostoyevsky, *The Brothers Karamazov,* from the chapter entitled "Rebellion," in the translation by David Magarshack in the Penguin Classics edition (New York: Penguin, 1958).

Chapter V: The Dying of the Light

The title of this chapter is borrowed from Dylan Thomas's poem, "Do Not Go Gentle into That Good Night." The story about Emil Brunner's exchange with an American student is told by J. Louis Martyn in "From Paul to Flannery O'Connor with the Power of Grace," *Katallagete* (Winter 1981) 13. Michael Deshe's poem was quoted in an editorial written by John Gittings in the British newspaper the *Guardian,* on January 27, 1995. Leni Yahil talks about Nazism as a counter-society striving toward death in her book on the Holocaust (see the notes to the Preface), p. 454. My characterization of Jesus as "the man who had thought to change the course of the world" echoes the famous words of Albert Schweitzer, *The Quest of the Historical Jesus* (New York: Macmillan Publishing Company, 1968; orig. 1906) 370–71. Martin Luther's exegesis of Jesus' citation of Psalm 22 from the cross is summarized by Paul Althaus, *The Theology of Martin Luther* (Philadelphia: Fortress, 1966) 206. I am aware of how problematical it is to cite Luther, whose anti-Semitic opinions in some ways anticipated those of the Nazis, in a book about the Holocaust—especially as summarized by Althaus, who in many ways compromised with Nazism (see Robert P. Ericksen, *Theologians Under Hitler: Gerhard Kittel, Paul Althaus, and Emmanuel Hirsch* [New Haven and London: Yale University Press, 1985] 79–119). But no one has written more powerfully than Luther about Jesus' experience of God-forsakenness on the cross. Elie Wiesel's story about the trial of God is described on p. vii of Robert McAffee Brown's introduction to Wiesel's play *The Trial of God* (New York: Schocken, 1995).

Chapter VI: It Is Finished!

For Eliach book, see notes to Chapter I. The passage from Toni Morrison's *Beloved* (London: Chatto & Windus, 1987) occurs on pp. 272–73.

Chapter VII: The Earthquake

The discussion of the theology of Rabbi Haim of Volozhin is from Emmanuel Levinas, "Judaism and Kenosis," in *In the Time of the Nations* (see the notes on Chapter II) 114–32. I have altered the translation of Levinas's French slightly in the interest of clarity. In the 1970s Hal Lindsey wrote a popular book called *Satan*

Is Alive and Well on Planet Earth (Grand Rapids: Zondervan, 1974; repr. New York: Bantam Books, 1984). The quotations from Dostoyevsky's *Brothers Karamazov* are, like those cited in Chapter IV, from the section entitled "Rebellion," which immediately precedes the "Grand Inquisitor." In view of his anti-Semitism, it is perhaps almost as risky to cite Dostoyevsky as it is to cite Luther and T. S. Eliot in sermons about the Holocaust; but see the illuminating essay by A. S. Steinberg, "Dostoevski and the Jews," in *The Jew: Essays from Martin Buber's Journal Der Jude, 1916–1928* (ed. Arthur A. Cohen; Tuscaloosa, Ala.: University of Alabama Press, 1980) 158–70. On the theory that the tearing of the Temple veil is not only a foreshadowing of the destruction of the Temple but also an act of divine mourning at Jesus' death, analogous to human mourners' tearing of their garments, see David Daube, *The New Testament and Rabbinic Judaism* (London: Athlone, 1956; repr. Peabody, Mass.: Hendrickson, 1994) 23–24. Besides the analogy with the High Priest's tearing of his garment in Matthew 26:65, which is mentioned by Daube, this interpretation is also supported by the fact that the rip goes from top to bottom. There is a certain analogy in rabbinic passages in which God, like a human king in mourning, tears his purple garment as a sign of his grief at the destruction of Jerusalem and its Temple *(Pesikta de Rav Kahana* 15:3; *Leviticus Rabbah* 6:5; *Lamentations Rabbah* 15:3). These passages may well allude to the destruction of the Temple's purple curtain (cf. 2 Chronicles 3:14; Josephus, *Jewish War* 5.212–13 on the purple color of the curtain). My comments on the difference between the God of Ivan Karamazov and the God of his brother Alyosha draw on remarks made by Bruce Ward at the University of Glasgow's Centre for Literature and Theology in a discussion of his paper "Dostoevsky and the Hermeneutics of Suspicion," which will appear in *Literature and Theology* 11 (1997). Dr. Ward also pointed out to me, after I had written this chapter, that when his own son died, Dostoyevsky was so distraught that he sought counsel at a monastery, where the spiritual director responded to the grief-stricken father by quoting the same biblical passage about Rachel weeping for her children that I have alluded to here. "That was the monk's only response; and Dostoevsky was so struck by it that he incorporated it a few years later in *The Brothers Karamazov* (in a chapter near the beginning called 'Devout Peasant Women')"; see Anna Dostoevsky, *Dostoevsky: Reminiscences* (trans. and ed. Beatrice Stillman; New York: Liveright, 1975) 291–94. The final words of this chapter have been adapted from one of the collects in the Episcopal *Book of Common Prayer*.

Final Thoughts

The Martin Buber–Karl Ludwig Schmidt dialogue is reprinted in Karl Ludwig Schmidt, *Neues Testament. Judentum. Kirche: Kleine Schriften Herausgegeben zu seinem 90. Geburtstag am 5. Februar 1981* (ed. Gerhard Sauter; Theologische Bücherei 69; München: Chr. Kaiser Verlag, 1981) 149–65. The English translation is from David McKain, ed., *Christianity: Some Non-Christian Appraisals* (Westport, Conn.: Greenwood Press, 1976) 186–87. Buber refers to Jesus as his "great [or elder] brother" in *Two Types of Faith* (New York: Collier Books/Macmillan Publishing Company, 1951) 12.